Why Did the Logician
Cross the Road?

Also Available From Bloomsbury

Why Did the Logician Cross the Road?

Finding Humor in Logical Reasoning

Stan Baronett

BLOOMSBURY ACADEMIC
LONDON • NEW YORK • OXFORD • NEW DELHI • SYDNEY

BLOOMSBURY ACADEMIC
Bloomsbury Publishing Plc
50 Bedford Square, London, WC1B 3DP, UK
1385 Broadway, New York, NY 10018, USA
29 Earlsfort Terrace, Dublin 2, Ireland

BLOOMSBURY, BLOOMSBURY ACADEMIC and the Diana logo are
trademarks of Bloomsbury Publishing Plc

First published in Great Britain 2021
Copyright © Stan Baronett, 2021

Stan Baronett has asserted his right under the Copyright, Designs and
Patents Act, 1988, to be identified as Author of this work.

Cover design by Louise Dugdale

A catalogue record for this book is available from the British Library.

Library of Congress Cataloging-in-Publication Data

Names: Baronett, Stan, author.
Title: Why did the logician cross the road? : finding humor in logical
reasoning / Stan Baronett.
Description: London, UK ; New York, NY, USA : Bloomsbury Academic, 2021. |
Includes bibliographical references and index. |
Identifiers: LCCN 2021006765 (print) | LCCN 2021006766 (ebook) | ISBN
9781350178908 (hb) | ISBN 9781350178915 (pb) | ISBN 9781350178922 (epdf)
| ISBN 9781350178939 (ebook)
Subjects: LCSH: Reasoning—Humor. | Logic—Humor.
Classification: LCC BC177 .B335 2021 (print) | LCC BC177 (ebook) | DDC
160.2/07—dc23
LC record available at https://lccn.loc.gov/2021006765
LC ebook record available at https://lccn.loc.gov/2021006766

ISBN: HB: 978-1-3501-7890-8
        PB: 978-1-3501-7891-5
        ePDF: 978-1-3501-7892-2
        eBook: 978-1-3501-7893-9

Typeset by RefineCatch Limited, Bungay, Suffolk
Printed and bound in Great Britain

To find out more about our authors and books visit www.bloomsbury.com
and sign up for our newsletters.

Contents

Preface

The goal of introducing philosophical thought through humor is not new. Several books have used humor to illustrate such topics as ethics, metaphysics, epistemology, religion, and politics. Those books presented great thinkers such as Plato, Aristotle, and Kant, while also offering insights into classic philosophical traditions such as rationalism, empiricism, and existentialism.

In this book, humor is used to introduce basic *logical reasoning* and its connection to real life. The important, interesting, and practical applications of logical reasoning are presented using jokes and stories. Humor can help us understand logic, and logic can help us understand humor.

While logical reasoning is typically presented and studied as an abstract subject—quite often through the use of a formal, symbolic language—it can in fact be shown to have a grounded and practical application. By combining jokes, stories, and ironic situations, logical reasoning is woven into the fabric of everyday experience. Humor can defuse the anxiety many people associate with abstract logical concepts. And since most people are good at remembering jokes and funny stories, they can readily grasp and recall the logical points that are illustrated.

So, in the best of all possible worlds, reading this book will help you understand some of the fundamentals of logical reasoning, and give you a few laughs. In the worst of all possible worlds, it will do neither. If the latter turns out to be the case, then blame Gottfried Leibniz—he's the one who said that this was the best of all possible worlds.

On the other hand, readers might experience a phenomenon similar to what Groucho Marx once wrote about regarding his friend's recently published book: "From the moment I picked up your book until I put it down, I was convulsed with laughter. Some day I intend reading it."

1

You Call That An Argument?

Logical reasoning and humor have an interesting relationship. Jokes often set up a plausible premise based on everyday experience. Once the basics of the story are set, our minds anticipate typical—and logical—endings based on patterns of experience gained throughout our lives. An effective joke may rely on an *unanticipated assumption* that leads to an *unexpected result*. The assumption changes the normal context of an everyday situation, so we are surprised by the ending. After all, we rely on our minds to predict the future, based on past experience. A complex mind that learns from experience, and builds a storehouse of regularly recurring patterns, is a great survival tool. But for a joke to be effective, the punch line has to be something our minds don't logically anticipate. The ending jolts our minds for a split second while we grasp the absurdity of the situation. Laughter is a release of the tension caused by an unexpected outcome. Laughter massages the logical mind.

In our daily routines, a sudden collapse of powers of prediction would be scary. But when we listen to a joke we are willing to suspend those powers. The unexpected punch line is not threatening because we know it is not a real-life situation and nothing is at stake. The joke lets us experience unpredictability safely, and reminds us that our powers of prediction are subject to the endless uncertainties of life, as the following story illustrates:

A philosophy teacher decides to try something different to test his students. "Today we are going to have a pop quiz." The students groan and grumble as they take out some paper to write.

The teacher lifts a chair, puts it on his desk and says, "I want you to apply what you have learned in this class and prove to me that the chair I placed on the desk does not exist."

While the rest of the class gets immediately busy writing elaborate essays using dubious philosophical ideas, one student remains surprisingly calm. The confident student hands in her paper, on which is written: "What chair?"

Diverse life experiences help us anticipate future events and recognize the logic of a situation. For purposes of understanding how logic works we can look at how our minds function on several levels. The first level concerns facts and the determination of truth. This function can be understood through a simple exercise. Read the following short sentence, and as soon as you finish *try not to decide whether the sentence is true or false*:

The Statue of Liberty is made of green cheese.

Okay, admit it. As soon as you read the sentence you knew it to be false. You did not have to think about it, and you could not stop the process because one part of your mind immediately determined that it was false. So, in a sense, your conscious self had no say in the matter, your knowing that it was false was a *mind-jerk* reaction. As this illustrates, one part of your mind is constantly working on determining whether the information you are receiving from the world is true or false.

But another part of your mind works differently. It deals with the *logical consequences* of information; in other words, what *follows from* that information. This part of the mind does *not* try to determine whether the information is true or false. Instead, it investigates whether one piece of information *follows from* other pieces. For example, suppose you are driving a car and you are about to enter an intersection where the light is green. Although you cannot see the cross-traffic light, you *infer* or *conclude* that it is red. But your conclusion could be wrong—the cross-traffic light could be malfunctioning. Given this, we say that your inference has an *uncertainty* to it.

When we receive information, we often begin anticipating where that information might lead. Depending on the situation, it is also natural to interpret the information as stemming from the context in which it occurs. For example, the following conversation might arise when a student goes to her instructor's office:

> "I have been thinking a lot about the consequences of our actions, and how the different moral theories you have introduced to us in our Ethics class are to be understood and applied to everyday situations. For example, I would like to know if it is always wrong to punish a person for something she didn't do?"
>
> The instructor says, "Yes, that would be wrong."
>
> The student says, "That's good to hear because I didn't do my homework."

The instructor interprets the student's question as indicating the student is taking the course seriously and is trying to work out how moral theories can be applied to an apparent hypothetical situation. Therefore, the instructor's answer is based on that interpretation. As we saw earlier, our minds work on several levels, and our conscious thoughts are only the tip of the iceberg compared to the vast amount of unconscious processing that goes on constantly in our brains.

When we watch a movie or read a novel, we often try to anticipate the ending. For example, as a murder mystery unfolds we might try to guess who did it, and we can make adjustments as more information and clues are revealed. This shows that we are actively assessing the significance of information, interpreting it, and judging which outcome is more likely to follow from the evidence currently at hand. Depending on the complexity of the story, we might change our minds several times until the answer is finally revealed. And we can be completely fooled by a surprise ending. This active process of deriving possible conclusions as a story unfolds also happens when we hear a comedian tell a joke, or when we read a funny story.

> Kelly hadn't seen her friend, Nancy, for several months, so she was surprised that Nancy seemed so sad. "What's wrong?" asked Kelly.
>
> "Three months ago my uncle died, but he left me $10,000 in his will," said Nancy.
>
> "I'm so sorry. Were you close?" asked Kelly.

"Not really. I was surprised that he left me any money at all. And then two months ago another uncle died, and he left me $25,000 in his will," said Nancy.

"Oh my, two uncles in two months, that's very strange," remarked Kelly.

"Yeah, and that's not all. Last month my aunt died and she left me $50,000 in her will," said Nancy.

"Gee, I don't know what to say. Three relatives died in three months, and they each left you money. That's incredible. No wonder you're so sad," Kelly said.

"Uh, huh. And then this month, nothing! Can you believe it?" cried Nancy.

Most people are surprised by the ending. Maybe you were surprised because as you were reading you were forming some ideas about where it was heading, however tentative those ideas might have been. Perhaps you were influenced by certain words or phrases, such as "Nancy seemed so sad." Perhaps you thought that Nancy was feeling somewhat undeserving of the inheritance because she said that she wasn't really close to the first uncle she mentioned. That idea might have influenced how you interpreted Nancy's relationship with the other two relatives who left her money, even though it wasn't explicitly said. When the source of Nancy's sadness is finally revealed there is a split second where we absorb the new information, and even though our ideas were wrong, the unanticipated ending allows us to laugh.

What's It All About?

Logic studies reasoning and arguments. An *argument* is a network of *statements* (sentences that are either true or false) in which the *premises* are intended to provide good reasons to accept the *conclusion*. Argument analysis concerns two main questions:

1. Are the premises true?
2. If the premises are true, do they support the conclusion?

The first question falls into the domain of fact, while the second is squarely in the sights of logic. Logic investigates the level of correctness of the reasoning found in arguments. Logical investigation of an argument begins after you learn how to recognize arguments when you are reading and when you are listening to others. Logic provides the tools and skills necessary to analyze other people's arguments; it also enables you to analyze objectively your own arguments, thereby anticipating challenges and criticisms.

Of course, the term "argument" also has a completely different meaning from the one we are describing:

> A couple have a heated argument one night which ends in their not talking to each other. Before going to sleep that night, Mike writes a note and leaves it on Clare's pillow: "I have an early meeting tomorrow, so be sure to wake me at 6 a.m."
>
> When Mike wakes up the next morning he sees that it is already past 8 a.m. He is about to leap out of bed when he sees a note by his pillow. The note reads: "It's 6 a.m. Time to wake up."

The story reveals one kind of relationship, strained as it might be. However, as you shall soon see, the strength of the *relationship between the premises and the conclusion of an argument* is a major concern of logic. Conclusions are statements that need support. For example, the following list of statements (which are either true or false) would need to be backed up by good arguments in order to be accepted:

- He is guilty of murder.
- You have diabetes.
- Your car needs a new transmission.
- We should spend more money on preschool education.
- Taxes should be raised.

Any of the above statements could be the conclusion of an argument. But since there is no reason to accept any of them at face value, we expect each of them to be supported by good reasons. Conclusions require the support of premises for their justification. For example, a prosecutor cannot simply say, "The defendant is guilty," and expect a jury to convict someone on the basis of that one statement. The prosecutor must provide strong support (evidence) to get the jury to agree that the defendant is guilty.

We create arguments for a variety of reasons. For example, if we are engaged in an interesting conversation we might be asked to think on our toes, to justify our position. Once an argument is in place (the premises and conclusion are clearly identified), then we can apply our logical analysis skills to investigate whether or not the premises offer strong support for the conclusion. Understanding the basics of logic enables you to determine whether an argument is strong or weak. Generally speaking, constructing strong arguments from scratch takes time. However, a few basic logical analysis skills can help you avoid simple mistakes in reasoning.

Statements

The term "statement" refers to a sentence occurring in a specific language. For example, the statement "Prunes are a natural laxative" is in English. Translated into other languages we get the following statements:

- La ciruela es un laxante natural.   (Spanish)
- Pflaumen sind ein natürliches Abführmittel.   (German)
- Les pruneaux sont un laxatif naturel.   (French)
- Plommon ni laxative asili.   (Swahili)

Although the statements are in different languages, *they all make the same assertion.* In other words, the statements all have the same meaning. Statements take the form of declarative sentences. As the name indicates, we *declare* that something is the case. When you declare or assert that something is the case, then your statement has a *truth value*—it is either true or false. And since each of the earlier declarative sentences about prunes make the same assertion, they all have the same truth value. If any of them is true, then all of them are true.

However, we don't have to know the truth value of a specific statement in order to accept that it has to be either true or false. For example, the statement, "A treasure chest is at the bottom of Lake Erie" is either true or false, even though we might never be in a position to decide the issue. The same holds for the statement, "My great-grandmother weighed exactly nine pounds at birth." The fact that it must be true or false does not depend on our being able to determine its truth value. However, there are many perfectly acceptable sentences that do not have a truth value, and therefore are not statements. Here are some examples:

- When were you born? (*Question*)
- Wash the car. (*Command*)
- Please, wash the car. (*Request*)
- Let's work together on the project. (*Proposal*)

Although they are all perfectly good sentences, none of them are statements; hence, they are neither true nor false. Sometimes a sentence might appear to be a statement, but it turns out not to be the case. The context in which a sentence occurs often provides clues to a speaker's or writer's intended meaning. For example, if you overhear someone say, "My darling, your skin is as soft as a newborn baby," you shouldn't run out and get a baby to do a scientific comparison. Therefore, paying attention to context is quite important in helping us to decide whether a sentence is being used as a statement.

Arguments

Arguments are created in order to establish support for a claim, so it is expected that the premises provide good reasons for accepting the conclusion. In addition, arguments should be truth-preserving, which means that if we start with true premises, then we should end with a true conclusion. This emphasis on truth requires that all premises and conclusions must be statements.

A logical analysis of an argument leaves emotion out of the equation. It relies solely on objective criteria and rationality. Arguments can be found everywhere. Most people expect to find arguments presented in courtroom battles between defense attorneys and prosecutors. Arguments are also present in medical cases to help a patient decide whether to have an operation, or to seek alternative treatment. In fact, patients often get a second or third opinion before deciding what to do based on the best evidence available. Although you might not realize it, arguments are just as likely to occur when a car mechanic gives you advice about your car. The mechanic might offer reasons to get your car engine rebuilt, or suggest a cheaper alternative, depending on how long you expect to keep the car. In addition, plumbers, electricians, engineers, carpenters, computer technicians, writers, teachers, office workers, sales people, bus and taxi drivers, and managers use arguments on a regular basis. Arguments are used to sell products, buy insurance, take a vacation, get training, how to raise a child, how to plan an estate, where to save or invest your money, to name only a few instances. And of course, arguments are most definitely found in political debates, and in ethical, religious, and cultural disputes. Arguments should be judged on logic, not on emotion. A clear, cool head can help you respond to challenges or objections.

Studying logical reasoning enables you to master many skills that can be used on a daily basis. It sharpens the ability to identify arguments, whether in written or oral form. Daily life rarely presents us with complete and perfectly-designed arguments. Instead, we usually have to separate the wheat from the chaff. Making matters worse, real-life arguments are often incomplete, so we must be able to reconstruct the final product.

Although every argument has premises intended to support a conclusion, not every set of sentences qualifies as an argument. A group of perfectly sensible sentences might simply be a set of opinions or beliefs. If nothing serves as a premise and nothing is a conclusion, then we don't have an argument. For example, here is something that people who have to pay an agent's fee might put in a last will:

Please respect my wish to to be cremated. Also, since my agent's contract stipulates that he gets fifteen percent of everything I have, give him that same percentage of my ashes.

The statement certainly lets us know how the person feels about a certain issue. Also, the sentences may be true or false with respect to her opinions. However, none of the sentences seem to offer any support for a conclusion. They are simply instructions that are meant to be carried out.

We currently have access to enormous amounts of information instantly at our fingertips. Searching for information and finding what we need has never been easier. For example, newspaper articles typically supply information about a situation by satisfying the "five w's of reporting": *who, what, where, when,* and *why.* Many newspaper articles do not offer arguments, thus, they don't generally conclude anything. However, arguments can be found on the editorial page. Readers send in their opinions, but occasionally they also offer arguments. Also, editors provide arguments for various social or political issues.

In everyday conversation, it is not always obvious that people are presenting an argument. However, we can analyze what they say to flesh out their reasoning process.

Michael gives his roommate, Dave, two ties for his birthday. Dave goes to his bedroom and puts on one of the ties. When he comes down smiling, Michael says, "Oh, so you don't like the other tie."

From the fact that Dave chose one of the ties to wear, Michael quickly concluded that Dave doesn't like the other tie. Michael's reasoning process included a general assumption: *If you don't wear something I give you, then you don't like it.* Although this may be correct in many cases, it is not always true, especially in this case where Dave can wear only one tie at a time. Based on Michael's assumption, whichever tie Dave chose to wear would lead to Michael's unwarranted conclusion.

Determining whether written material contains an argument can sometimes pose special problems. Although some writers clearly establish their arguments, other writers either hide their meaning or fail to spell out in detail their arguments. Since we generally are not in a position to ask writers to explain their intentions, the material can be hard to analyze adequately. If we have some knowledge and experience of the topic that a writer is discussing, then we can reconstruct the arguments by drawing on that knowledge. Since every argument has a conclusion, we can begin by looking for some simple conclusion indicator words or phrases, such as *therefore, thus, so,* and *it follows that.* When no obvious conclusion indicator words are available, then we can use other means to identify the conclusion, such as placing the word "therefore" in front of a statement to see if it is the conclusion.

The recognition of premises follows a similar process. Premise indicator words or phrases include *because, since, given that, assuming that.* If no obvious premise indicator words are available, then you can use another technique: place the word "because" in front of a sentence to see if it is a premise. Once again, context and familiarity with the issue can help. The following is an example of an argument without premise or conclusion indicator words:

> During check-in at an airport a passenger says, "I would like you to send one of my suitcases to Miami and the other to Los Angeles."
> The check-in agent smiles and says, "I'm sorry, we can't do that."
> The passenger replies, "You did it the last time I flew."

The passenger's reasoning is this: *Because* the airline sent one of my suitcases to Miami and the other to Los Angeles the last time I flew, *therefore*, I would like the airline to send one of my suitcases to Miami and the other to Los Angeles this time.

Explanations

Although we can generally rely on premise indicators to help recognize arguments, there are exceptions. For example, although the word "because" can indicate the presence of a premise, it can also be placed in front of an *explanation*, which is not an argument. An explanation functions as a way of describing how or why something happened. A simple example can reveal the difference between an *argument* and an *explanation*. Imagine that a person arrives at work three hours late, and the office manager says the following:

> *Because* you arrived so late for work, I can conclude that you are not serious about keeping your position with this company.

In this setting, the word "because" indicates that the office manager is going to provide a reason for concluding something about the employee's motivation. Now suppose that the person who was late to work responds as follows:

> I was late to work *because* my daughter woke up this morning with a fever and I had to take her to the clinic. We had to wait for nearly two hours until a doctor could see us.

In this setting, the word "because" is used to indicate that an *explanation* is being offered. The person does not dispute the fact that she was late to work; she is simply *explaining* why it happened.

Many things appear puzzling until an adequate explanation is put forward. The next story illustrates how a simple explanation can clear up a seemingly strange behavior:

> A young boy and his sister are walking by their neighbor's house. The neighbor and his wife are sitting on the front steps, and the husband says, "This kid never learns, no matter how many times I play the same game with him. Watch this."
>
> He calls the boy over and proceeds to put a dollar bill in one hand and two quarters in the other hand. He tells the boy, "You can take what is in either hand." The boy quickly takes the two quarters, smiles and walks away. The neighbor laughs, shakes his head, and goes inside to get a couple of drinks. As the boy and his sister walk away, the sister asks, "Why did you take the two quarters instead of the dollar? Don't you know which is worth more?"
>
> "Sure I do," said the boy, "But as soon as I take the dollar the game is over."

Truth and Logic

Argument analysis consists of two parts. The first part concerns *truth content analysis*: *Are the premises true or false?* (An argument can certainly have one premise, but I will typically use the plural "premises" when discussing argument analysis.) The second part concerns *logical analysis*: *Assuming the premises are true, then what follows?* Mastering logical analysis requires the active separation of these two parts, which require radically different processes.

Truth content analysis requires gathering reliable information to determine whether the premises are true. In contrast to this, logical analysis investigates whether the conclusion *follows from* the premises, *assuming the premises are true*. Logical analysis, therefore, requires a suspension of the judgment of the truth content of the premises because the logical focus is an entirely separate question. For example, it is very easy to misinterpret visual evidence and then use it to infer an unjustified conclusion. To illustrate this, consider the story of two inexperienced aviators who were flummoxed on their final approach to an airport:

Pilot   Wow, that's the shortest runway I've ever seen.

Co-pilot   Yeah, but look how wide it is.

Both the pilot and co-pilot *assumed* they were on the correct landing approach to the airport. Given this assumption, they *concluded* that the runway was short but wide. We can see that *if* the assumption were true, then the conclusion follows. But since the conclusion is false, the premise must be false—they were *not* on the correct landing approach to the airport.

To help you understand how truth content and logical analysis differ, let's look at how we process other kinds of information. The sense of sight and the sense of smell are two distinct functions. We do not expect our eyes to sense a flower's fragrance, and we do not expect our noses to sense the flower's color. (But guess what? There are some people who experience *synesthesia*, a rare condition where a person might, for example *hear colors*. Researchers conjecture that synesthesia results from interconnections between different parts of the brain that are activated by a sensory stimulus. In other words, a stimulus that activates one particular sense in most people may activate several senses in someone who has synesthesia.) Many people unconsciously shut their eyes in order to heighten the sensation of a pleasant aroma. Closing the eyes can also help us concentrate on hearing something more distinctly. Similarly, when we are focusing on the *logic* of an argument, we need to temporarily suspend our judgment of the *truth content*.

The process under discussion is similar to other types of reasoning, such as simple arithmetic. What happens when children begin learning addition? Typically, the teacher uses visual cues, such as fruit or toys. For example, the teacher might hold one apple in each hand and ask the class to add them up. It all sounds so simple, right? It is once you learn to separate the abstract mathematics of the problem from its truth content. An elementary teacher once reported a story that is quite typical of the learning process involved in addition. She said that one day she gave two cookies to each student at the beginning of the class. When it came time to do addition, she called on Sam and said, "You have the two cookies I gave you, and Sophie has the two cookies I gave her. So, Sam, tell me how many cookies you and Sophie have all together?" To the teacher's astonishment, Sam began sobbing. "It's okay if you can't do the addition, Sam, don't cry." Through his tears, Sam said that he didn't know how to answer the question because he had already eaten his two cookies. Sam confused the *truth content* of the teacher's claim that he had two cookies with the math (and *logical*) question that required Sam to simply *assume* that he had two cookies. It is easy to forget that it often takes a considerable amount of time to learn to think abstractly. Of course, getting the correct answer depends on how you go about solving a simple math problem:

"Why do you believe that $2 + 2 = 5$?"

"Because every time I add 2 to another 2, I get 5."

"Show me how you do it."

"First I take a rope and tie two knots in it. Then I take another rope and tie two knots in it. When I tie the two ropes together I get five knots."

The two ropes weren't the only things that got tied up in knots. To begin an objective analysis of an argument, we need to *temporarily assume* that the premises are true in order to analyze the *logical relationship* to the conclusion. This allows us to concentrate on the important logical questions at hand. In the rope example, we see that tying the two knotted ropes together smuggled in a further knot; in other words, it added an *unjustified* additional premise.

In everyday life, we often say something like the following: "Okay, assuming that what you have told me is true, let's see if your argument holds water." This means that we will analyze the argument under the best case scenario, namely assuming the premises are true. Adhering to this procedure focuses our attention and analysis squarely on the logical question of the strength of an argument.

> A priest, an engineer, and a logician are stranded on an island with lots of canned food, but with no tools to open the cans.
> The minister says, "Let us pray," but of course the cans do not open.
> The engineer says, "Let's build a fire and heat the cans until they burst open." But they quickly realize they have no matches or lighters.
> The logician says, "First, let's *assume* that we have a can opener ..."

Temporarily assuming that the premises are true certainly helps us to analyze the *logical* relationship in an argument. However, we also need to explore whether the assumptions are warranted. In the example above, all of the stranded people would agree that *if* they had a can opener, then they could easily open the cans. Although the conclusion follows logically, their problem is they lack a real can opener.

Giving the benefit of the doubt to people occurs in a variety of settings. It can also lead to humorous outcomes:

> Four college students devise a plan that will enable them to miss the midterm exam, but still ensure that their instructor will allow them to take a make-up exam. This way they hope to be able to gain some valuable information about the exam from students who took it on time.

The four students go to the instructor the day after the exam. They say that on their way to the exam their car got a flat tire, but they had no spare tire to replace it. They had to wait for someone to bring them a new tire, so they couldn't make it to class on time.

The instructor agrees to let them take the exam the next day. After getting some information about the exam from classmates, the four felt well-prepared. The next day in her office the instructor hands them the exam. Here is the first question: "Which tire was flat?"

Puzzles

"Thought puzzles" appear at the end of each chapter, and they draw on logical thinking. None of them require any deep technical knowledge. Instead, they can be solved by close attention to the details and exploring logical possibilities. For the most part they will be minimalist puzzles, so the details are important. Just try to focus on the information before you attempt a solution.

Sometimes our thinking gets stuck in a rut. This can happen if we miss seeing alternative ways of understanding a problem while we are locked into one way of reasoning about a problem. Heading down a wrong path can lead to being stuck in a logical loop. We get out of the loop when we suddenly "see" the solution, and our minds light up with the correct answer (the wonderful *Aha!* experience). But don't worry—answers and explanations for all the puzzles are provided at the back of the book.

The Cake Puzzle

Suppose that you are presented with a cake and are told that you must cut the cake into two equal pieces with one slice of a knife. You find this to be not much of a challenge, and proceed to cut the cake as directed:

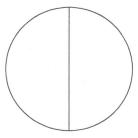

Having successfully cut the cake into two equal pieces, you are then directed to cut the cake into four equal pieces with just one additional slice of the knife. Again, you do not find this difficult:

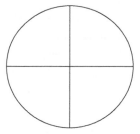

Now the plot thickens. You are hereby directed to cut the cake into *eight equal parts*, again with only one additional slice of the knife. Can you do it?

That Comes In Two Flavors

Logicians have devised several categories for arguments, but as a way to get started we will concentrate on deductive and inductive arguments. Let's start with deductive arguments. A *deductive argument* is one in which it is asserted that the conclusion *follows necessarily* from the premises. Since the assertion may turn out to be incorrect, we can further define deductive arguments. A *valid* deductive argument requires the following: *Assuming that all the premises are true, it must be impossible for the conclusion to be false.* Since logical analysis of a deductive argument focuses on whether the conclusion follows necessarily from the premises, we can ask the following: "Does the truth of the premises *guarantee* the truth of the conclusion?" A deductive argument in which the conclusion does follow necessarily from the premises is a *valid* argument. On the other hand, a deductive argument in which the conclusion *does not* follow necessarily from the premises is an *invalid* argument. Armed with this definition, let's look at an instance of everyday reasoning:

> A man wants to sit down next to a woman at a park bench, but is afraid to when he sees a large dog next to the woman.
> "Excuse me," he says. "Does your dog bite?"
> The woman smiles and says, "No, he doesn't."
> The man sits down, and the dog immediately bites him on the leg.
> "I thought you said that your dog doesn't bite," screams the man.
> "He doesn't," says the woman. "But that's not my dog."

So what went wrong? What did the man *assume*, and what did he *conclude*? First, he assumed that the woman's claim that her dog doesn't bite was true. Second, he assumed that the large dog next to the woman was her dog. Here is his argument:

Premise 1: That woman's dog doesn't bite.
Premise 2: The large dog next to the woman is her dog.
Conclusion: The large dog next to the woman will not bite me.

Under the assumption that both premises are true, the conclusion follows necessarily, so it is a valid argument. But how can a valid argument lead to a false conclusion? This example illustrates the main point that we have been discussing, namely, the difference between the *truth content* of statements and the question of what *logically follows from* those statements. Logically speaking, *if* Premise 1 *and* Premise 2 of the above argument are both true, then the conclusion follows necessarily. But in the above example the conclusion turned out to be false (the dog really did bite him), so we know that *at least* one of the premises is false (in this case it is Premise 2). Therefore, whether an argument is valid or invalid depends solely on what logically follows *if all the premises are true*. And that's why the man's argument was valid, but he got bit anyway.

Here is another illustration of the same point:

Premise 1: If I have exactly ten million dollars in my checking account, then I am a millionaire.
Premise 2: I have exactly ten million dollars in my checking account.
Conclusion: I am a millionaire.

Once again, under the assumption that both premises are true, the conclusion follows necessarily, so it is a valid argument. In other words, the validity of the argument guarantees that the conclusion is true *under the assumption that both premises are true*. However, if either of the premises turn out to be false, then the conclusion is no longer logically guaranteed to be true. We can all agree that *if* I truly have exactly ten million dollars in my checking account, then I am a millionaire. But if Premise 2 is false, then *the conclusion no longer follows necessarily*; in other words, *the conclusion might be true or false*. Two examples can illustrate this point.

Example A: If I have sixty million dollars in my checking account, then although Premise 2 is false, the conclusion is *true* (I am a millionaire).

Example B: If I have only $20 in my checking account, and I have no other assets, then the conclusion is *false* (I am *not* a millionaire).

This is why a valid argument means only that *under the assumption that both premises are true does the conclusion follow necessarily.*

Some people are dismayed by this result. It is common to hear the following complaint: "What good is a valid argument if it only allows us to claim that the conclusion is true under the *assumption* that *all* the premises are true? I want an argument to make sure the conclusion turns out to be *factually* true, too." This seems like a reasonable request. In fact, logicians have a perfectly reasonable answer to this request. If you want an argument that is both logically impeccable and has a true conclusion, then you need a *sound* argument. This is where *truth content* analysis does have a role. If our logical analysis of an argument determines that it is valid, we can then apply truth content analysis. If the truth content analysis of the premises shows that they are true, then the argument is *sound*. On the other hand, if the argument is invalid, or if *at least* one of the premises is false, then the argument is *unsound*. Connecting these distinctions back to the man who got bit by the dog, we can now see that whereas his argument was indeed valid, it was ultimately unsound, one of the premises he *assumed* to be true was in fact false.

We know that the premises of an argument are intended to support a conclusion, and in many cases, an argument's premises might seem to lead logically in one direction. However, it is also possible that two people might accept the same premises and yet derive completely different conclusions.

A pessimistic old man watches a young girl pick up a small struggling fish and gently place it back in the ocean. The old man approaches the girl and says, "I'm sorry to tell you, but what you did is a waste of time. Millions of fish get stuck on land and eventually die, gasping for air. So your act of placing that one fish back into the ocean does not make any difference."

The girl smiles and says, "It does for that fish."

Although the young girl accepted the pessimist's premises, she was able to derive a distinctly different conclusion. Let's hope that she retains her optimism, and her reasoning acumen, throughout her life.

We can now turn our attention to inductive arguments. In contrast to a deductive argument, an *inductive argument* is one in which it is asserted that the conclusion is *highly likely to be true, assuming the premises are true*. Inductive arguments get analyzed by asking two questions: First, *assuming* the premises are true, how *likely* is the conclusion to be true? Second, are the premises true? If logical analysis of an inductive argument reveals that the conclusion is highly likely to be true, assuming the premises are true, then it is a *strong* argument. On the other hand, if logical analysis of an inductive argument reveals that the conclusion is *not* highly likely to be true, assuming the premises are true, then it is a *weak* argument. As you can see, the words "strong" and "weak" are quite different from "valid" and "invalid."

If we add truth content analysis to the results of the logical analysis of an inductive argument, then we get two more designations. An argument is *cogent* only if both of the following requirements have been met: First, the argument is strong, and second, all of the premises are true. An argument is *uncogent* if either one, or both, of the following occur: the argument is weak, or the argument has at least one false premise.

Inductive arguments are readily found in everyday life, and especially in science, due to the fact that scientific research is an on-going process where new evidence can change our knowledge of how the world works. In order to decide whether an argument is deductive or inductive, it sometimes helps to consider the intent of the argument. Does the person who posed this argument intend the conclusion to follow with necessity or just with high probability? This line of thinking works best when we are familiar with the person making the argument or when the argument seems to head clearly in one direction.

Here are two arguments to consider (the premises are above the horizontal line and the conclusion is below it):

A. All dogs are mammals.
   <u>All mammals are intelligent.</u>
   All dogs are intelligent.

B. A few cars are worth $1,000,000.
   <u>I own a car.</u>
   My car is probably worth $1,000,000.

For argument A, *if* the premises are assumed to be true, then the conclusion follows necessarily, so it can be classified as deductive. (It is clearly valid, but do you think it is sound?) For argument B, the conclusion is not intended to follow with necessity (the term "probably" alerts us to that). Therefore, argument B is best classified as inductive (and *weak* because even if we assume the premises are true, the conclusion is unlikely to be true).

How would you assess the next example?

There is one sure way to discover if a politician is honest—just ask him straight out. If he says "Yes," then you immediately know he's a crook.

This example illustrates another point. Since many everyday arguments leave out important information, we are often forced to assume a lot of additional information that has not been made explicit. This means that we might have to reconstruct several possible alternatives and analyze each of them separately. This realization illustrates why you should make your arguments as clear as possible. First, it makes it easier for a listener or reader to understand your argument; second, it makes it easier for you to anticipate criticism, and thus create a better argument.

There is another important difference between deductive and inductive arguments. Deduction has an all-or-nothing outcome; induction doesn't. A deductive argument is either valid or invalid; there is no such thing as a semi-valid or partially invalid argument. The only way two valid arguments can be further distinguished is whether one is sound and the other is not. Otherwise all valid arguments are equal. In contrast to this, inductive arguments are definitely not all-or-nothing. One inductive argument can be *stronger* or *weaker* than another depending on the relative likelihood that the two conclusions are true, if the premises are assumed to be true.

Deductive logic is also called "formal logic," because it ultimately leads to the "form" of an argument, which is best represented by symbols rather than words (hence the term "symbolic logic"). Induction falls under the general heading "informal logic," because the determination of the amount of uncertainty involved cycles back to our knowledge of the world.

Since premises and conclusions must be statements, it is perfectly appropriate to refer to them as either true or false. However, an argument is *not* a statement; it is a special kind of network of statements. Therefore, it would be incorrect to label an argument as true or false. When we say that an argument is valid or invalid, or strong or weak, we are referring to the *logical relationship* between the premises and the conclusion. And because a logical relationship is not another statement, it is incorrect to label it as true or false. We can classify an argument as valid or invalid or strong or weak, but *not* true or false.

Certainty and Uncertainty

The quest for certainty has been a recurrent theme throughout human history. Logical analysis of deductive arguments reveals that at least one kind of certainty is achievable—*logical certainty.* If you want the conclusion of your argument to follow necessarily from the premises, then construct a valid argument. Although logical certainty is a worthy goal, we should not expect it of every argument. Everyday reasoning typically forces us to consider how to deal with *uncertainty.* A normal everyday setting can reveal how an unexpected conclusion can emerge from an ordinary conversation.

> A kindergarten class goes on a class outing to see a police station. The police officer conducting the tour points to a wall and says, "Kids, those are photographs of the ten most wanted criminals we are looking for."
>
> One small girl asks the police officer, "How come you didn't just hold on to them when you took their pictures?"

The girl's question seems quite reasonable. After all, she was told that the police are now looking for the criminals. She assumed that *if* the criminals were under arrest when the photos were taken, then they were obviously in police custody. From these pieces of information, she concluded that the police simply failed to hold on to the criminals when the pictures were taken.

After you master a few of the basic logic skills presented in this book, if you come across a real-life argument that appears to be deductive, then you can determine whether it is valid or invalid, and whether it is sound or unsound. If it seems that the argument is inductive, then you can decide (based on the degree of probability involved) if it is strong or weak, and whether it is cogent or uncogent.

For practical purposes, it is often useful to apply deductive analysis first because we often misjudge the strength of arguments. Some arguments can be deceptive and appear at first glance to be valid, so deductive analysis can clarify the issue. To show that an argument is invalid requires revealing the *possibility* of a false conclusion following from premises assumed to be true. This ability can assist us in thinking of how damaging these possibilities are, and if the argument can be salvaged. Classifying arguments as either deductive or inductive does not mean that these are the only two choices. The main point of this dual classification scheme is to show that a good way of looking at arguments is whether they are meant to achieve logical certainty, or if they are dealing with uncertainty.

We have all been involved in casual conversations that start out with a simple question or idea, but that soon lead to a series of inferences and logical analysis. The following shows a nice case of extended reasoning:

One night on a camping trip, Sherlock Holmes wakes Dr. Watson and asks the good doctor a question: "What do you see when you look up?"

"I see millions of stars," answers Watson.

"Good. Now tell me what you can infer from that fact."

"I can infer that there are billions of galaxies each containing billions of stars."

"Very good. Go on."

"There must be billions and billions of exoplanets, which astronomers define as planets that orbit around other stars. Further, since there is life on our planet, the chance of there being life on some exoplanet is high."

"I see. Quite well done, Watson. But you are overlooking one obvious inference."

"What is that?"

"Someone has stolen our tent!"

In the Arthur Conan Doyle stories, Holmes often said to Watson, "You *see*, but you do not *observe*." To explain the distinction, Holmes asked Watson if he knew how many steps led up to their second floor apartment. Watson admitted that he didn't know. According to Holmes, although Watson had *seen* (and climbed) the steps hundreds of times, he had not *observed* them. In contrast, Holmes knew that there were seventeen steps, because he had both seen and observed. The ability to pay close attention to details and apply reasoning techniques are skills that enable detectives, scientists, mechanics, computer programmers, physicians, and anyone attempting to solve a problem to create and analyze arguments.

Take That

Logic and truth content are the two basic components of argument analysis. Most people understand how to evaluate truth content because the education process is heavily devoted to learning what is true. The teaching of facts comprises the largest part of our basic education. But then you go to college, where the professor's job is to point out just how much you don't know. The illusion of understanding is further revealed as you proceed from undergraduate to graduate school. By the time you get a Ph.D. the veil of ignorance has been completely stripped away.

Logic and truth content can be illustrated by the use of *counterexamples*. Imagine that someone states the following: "No one is taller than eight feet." If we discovered someone who is over eight feet (this could be verified easily), then concrete evidence would exist showing that the statement was false. The evidence would act as a counterexample to the statement, and it concerns the truth content of a statement.

A counterexample to an *argument* is a different creature because it deals with the logic of an argument and not its truth content. The logic of an argument revolves around the relationship between the premises and the conclusion. Therefore, a counterexample to an argument must be able to clearly and precisely show that it is *possible* for true premises to lead to a false conclusion. This process emphasizes the rational aspect of developing counterexamples, a process that can be easily overlooked.

Counterexamples have vastly different effects on deductive and inductive arguments. Since deductive arguments have an all-or-nothing aspect (valid or invalid), a single counterexample is sufficient to show that a deductive argument is invalid. This is not surprising because there are no degrees of validity or invalidity. However, it is easy to miss the mark when struggling to find a good counterexample. The next story clearly illustrates how wishful thinking can supersede good reasoning.

> My mom says that the more I learn, the more I will know. But the more I know, the more I'm likely to forget. And the more I forget, the less I'll know. So, why should I bother learning anything?

On the other hand, since inductive arguments have ranges of strength, a single counterexample does not necessarily have a drastic effect on the overall strength of the argument. The amount of damage to an inductive argument depends on the relevance of the counterexample, and it can often require several counterexamples to severely weaken an inductive argument. These considerations clearly reveal major differences between deductive and inductive arguments.

A counterexample to an argument must directly expose a flaw in the relationship between the premises and the conclusion. As such, it does not address directly the truth content of the statements that make up the original argument. A simple example can easily show this distinction. Imagine that you were given information regarding two cars.

1. Car A has been driven fewer than 50,000 miles.
2. Car B has been driven fewer than 100,000 miles.

Would you be justified in concluding the following?

> *Premise 1*: Car A has been driven fewer than 50,000 miles.
> *Premise 2*: Car B has been driven fewer than 100,000 miles.
> *Conclusion*: Car A has been driven fewer miles than Car B.

Our logical analysis will focus on the relationship between the premises and the conclusion. If the two premises are assumed to be true, do they guarantee that the conclusion is true? Does a counterexample exist? This prompts us to investigate the relationship between the two premises and the conclusion. It is clear that these questions require radically different answers from the investigation of the truth content of the premises. An analogy might prove helpful here. When we discuss a romantic relationship between two people we know, it is quite common to use terms such as, *strong, supportive, healthy, shaky, weak,* and *on the rocks,* to name just a few. Similarly, logical analysis requires an assessment of the logical relationship between the premises and the conclusion.

Let's apply some possibilities to the argument about the cars. Suppose Car A has been driven 43,000 miles, and Car B has been driven 89,000 miles. In this case, the two premises are true and so is the conclusion. Let's try another possibility. Suppose Car A has been driven 43,000 miles, and Car B has been driven 27,000 miles. Since Premise 2 stated that Car B has been driven fewer than 100,000 miles, and since 27,000 miles is fewer than 100,000 miles, this is a legitimate possibility. In this case, both Premise 1 and Premise 2 are true, but the conclusion is false. This simple, but effective analysis has revealed a counterexample. The important thing to realize is that the *logical relationship* of an argument can, and must, be analyzed by purely logical means.

The following is a good example of how it is possible to take what is given and derive an *unexpected conclusion.* During the time of the United States' military engagement in Vietnam, the Soviet Union was supplying arms and aid to North Vietnam.

During the height of the Vietnam War, Ho Chi Minh sent a telegram to Moscow pleading for more support. A message was sent back from Moscow explaining that since it had been a particularly harsh winter throughout the Soviet Union, help could not be sent. The message ended this way: "You will have to tighten your belts."

Ho Chi Minh sent a return telegram: "Send belts."

Logical Possibilities

Imagine a case in which we have the following information:

1. A die has been thrown.
2. There are six sides on the die.
3. Each of the six sides has written on it one of the numerals 1-6, and no two sides have the same numeral.
4. This is an honest game.

You are asked to guess what number came up. If your guess is "6" the resulting argument is as follows:

1. A die has been thrown.
2. There are six sides on the die.
3. Each of the six sides has written on it one of the numerals 1-6, and no two sides have the same numeral.
4. <u>This is an honest game.</u>
   The number 6 came up.

If all four premises are assumed to be true, then a counterexample can be established easily by acknowledging that any of the other five numbers coming up is just as possible. These five possibilities can be considered as counterexamples to the argument. Purely for analysis sake, if the argument were considered to be deductive, then it would be invalid. If it were considered to be inductive, then it would be weak, since the conclusion has only a 1/6 chance of being true, assuming the premises are true.

Now suppose we are told that what came up is an even number. How does this new information affect the logical analysis? This is a new premise, so let's add it to the argument:

1. A die has been thrown.
2. There are six sides on the die.
3. Each of the six sides has written on it one of the numerals 1-6, and no two sides have the same numeral.
4. This is an honest game.
5. <u>The number that came up is an even number.</u>
   The number 6 came up.

A counterexample can still be given because any one of the three possible even numbers might have come up. Again, for analysis sake, if the argument were considered to be deductive, then it would be invalid. If it were considered to be inductive, then it would be weak, since the conclusion has only a 1/3 chance of being true, assuming the premises are true.

Suppose further that we are told that what came up is a number greater than 4. How would this affect the results of the logical analysis? Let's look at the resulting argument:

1. A die has been thrown.
2. There are six sides on the die.
3. Each of the six sides has written on it one of the numerals 1-6, and no two sides have the same numeral.
4. This is an honest game.
5. The number that came up is an even number.
6. <u>The number that came up is greater than 4.</u>
   The number 6 came up.

Premise 6 eliminates two of the three even numbers (if it is greater than 4, then it cannot be either 2 or 4). Therefore, assuming all six premises are true, then the argument is valid, and no counterexample exists. Since it is valid there is no need to consider its "strength" relative to it being an inductive argument. This example illustrates that it is possible to add new information in order to create a valid argument. Of course, you must always be careful not to add premises that are false, because doing so will create an unsound argument.

Here is an example where new information led to a drastic revision of what was assumed to be true:

> Sophie spotted a new employee looking helpless and confused in front of the paper shredder, so she decided to help.
>
> "Here, let me show you how the machine works," said Sophie. "It's really quite simple. You just put the documents in here and then hit this button." She then demonstrated the process.
>
> After the machine stopped the new employee said, "Thanks a lot. But where do the copies come out?"

As indicated by the story, there are times when new evidence causes us to question the truth of what we have previously assumed to be true. Sophie assumed that since the new employee was standing in front of the paper shredder, then the documents were meant to be shredded. On the other hand, the new employee assumed that she was standing in front of the copy machine. Both assumptions were wrong, but the two people didn't realize that until the new employee asked where the copies came out.

Here is another example of conflicting assumptions leading to unexpected results.

> A police officer stops a man driving a convertible with a zebra in the back seat. The officer says, "I'll let you go this time if you promise to take the zebra to the zoo."
>
> "Okay, sure," says the man.
>
> The next day the police officer sees the same man with the zebra. The officer stops him again and says, "Look sir, I told you to take the zebra to the zoo."
>
> "I did as you suggested," says the man. "But for a change, today I thought I'd take the zebra to the beach."

The story works because our assumption is the same as the police officer's, namely, "take the zebra to the zoo" means give the zebra to the zoo. The man interpreted the phrase as meaning "give the zebra an outing at the zoo." The humor results from our assumption being upended by an unexpected shift in the meaning of a simple phrase.

Categorical Arguments

Aristotle provided foundational support for *categorical logic* which concerns the relationships between classes of objects (also referred to as *categories* or *sets*). A simple definition of a *class* is "a set of objects." An example of a famous categorical statement is "All humans are mortal." Being an astute philosopher, logician, and scientist, Aristotle tried to harmonize science and logic. In fact, Aristotle thought that whereas scientific experiments provide specific cases of knowledge, logic enlarges our knowledge by ensuring that our inferences are logically valid. The prevailing notion of science during Aristotle's time rested on the idea of classification. It was thought that scientific knowledge grows when we are able to classify a group of objects as a subclass of another that is better known. Thus, empirical research meshes with logic, and we impart knowledge by relating what we have learned through experience.

Logical argument analysis starts with the *assumption* of true premises and proceeds to the investigation of the *possibility* of a false conclusion. We follow this procedure when determining the validity or invalidity of a categorical argument. For example, consider this argument:

All humans are mortal creatures.
<u>All mammals are mortal creatures.</u>
All humans are mammals.

Upon reading the argument, it is quite normal for most people to recognize immediately that the premises and the conclusion are true. This quick determination results from our minds automatically performing a *truth content analysis*, resulting in many people judging the argument to be *valid*. However, since evaluating the *strength* of an argument requires a *logical analysis,* if we instead focus on *truth content analysis*—whether we believe the information is true or false, or whether we simply agree with the conclusion—then our judgment may be influenced by that determination.

Although a quick assessment of an argument is often the result of a truth content analysis, it can negatively impact our *logical* reasoning skills. Many experiments have shown that when subjects are asked to determine whether arguments—similar to the argument above— were valid or invalid, many subjects mistakenly judged *invalid arguments* with *believable conclusions* to be *valid.* The subjects also mistakenly judged *valid arguments* with *unbelievable conclusions* to be *invalid.* Remember our mantra: Validity and invalidity are *not* determined by a truth content analysis of the statements that make up the argument; it is determined by a logical analysis—*assuming* the premises are true, is it *possible* for the conclusion to be false? To help us undertake the logical analysis, we can reveal the *form* of the above argument by letting H = *humans,* C = *mortal creatures,* and M = *mammals*:

All H are C.
All M are C.
All H are M.

We know that an invalid argument *cannot guarantee* that true premises will always lead to a true conclusion. So, let's see if we can create a counterexample using simple terms. Here are three simple terms that just happen to be walking by: let H = *apples,* C = *fruit,* and M = *oranges.* After substitution into the form of the argument we get this:

All apples are fruit.	*True*
All oranges are fruit.	*True*
All apples are oranges.	*False*

The counterexample clearly shows the *possibility of true premises leading to a false conclusion*; therefore, the argument is *invalid.* This illustrates the importance of learning how to critically and logically analyze information and arguments.

Okay, we have just enough time to do one more analysis. Consider this argument:

> All humans are mortal creatures.
> All mortal creatures are mammals.
> All humans are mammals.

It looks the same as the earlier argument, doesn't it? In fact, the first premise and the conclusion are identical, but the terms in the second premise have been reversed. As before, the first step of the *logical analysis* is to reveal the argument form. As before, let H = *humans*, C = *mortal creatures*, and M = *mammals*:

> All H are C.
> All C are M.
> All H are M.

For fun (okay, maybe a weird kind of fun), let's try substituting the terms we used earlier: let H = *apples*, C = *fruit*, and M = *oranges*. After substitution into the form of the argument we get this:

All apples are fruit.	*True*
All fruit are oranges.	*False*
All apples are oranges.	*False*

This shows the *possibility of a false conclusion, but not all the premises are true.* Therefore, this substitution of terms in the argument form *does not* show that the argument is invalid. In fact, it is impossible to get all true premises and a false conclusion with this argument form. Let's see why.

The first premise of the argument form asserts that every H is a C. Okay, let's *assume* that is true. The second premise asserts that every C is an M. Let's *assume* that is true, too. Now *if* every H is a C, and every C is an M, then *it follows necessarily* that every H is an M. The argument is valid, and no counterexample exists.

The Start-Finish Puzzle

You signed up to compete in two five-mile races on consecutive days. It is an unusual two races because on the first day you run from the "Start" banner and end at the "Finish" banner, but on the second day you run the race in the opposite direction; you start at the "Finish" banner and end at the "Start" banner. Both races begin at exactly 9:00 a.m. each day, The first day you are feeling pretty strong but you run a bit too fast, and although you finish in 27 minutes, your right thigh muscle begins to hurt. Nevertheless, you decide to run the next day. The race starts once again at 9:00 a.m., but since the pain is considerable you cannot run very fast, so it takes you 78 minutes to finish. Upon reflection, you suddenly realize that during the second race you passed one spot at the exact same time that you passed it when you ran the first race.

Question: *Is it correct that during the second race you passed one spot at the exact same time that you passed it when you ran the first race?*

I've Been Meaning To Tell You

Language is a tool, but even the best tools can be misused intentionally or unintentionally. Language can be clear or it can be murky. We often struggle to say just the right thing at the right time, and sometimes we fail. Lewis Carroll's *Alice's Adventures in Wonderland* offers a nice example of how we can get entangled in language:

March Hare   ...Then you should say what you mean.

Alice   I do; at least—at least I mean what I say—that's the same thing, you know.

Mad Hatter   Not the same thing a bit! Why, you might just as well say that "I see what I eat" is the same as "I eat what I see!"

March Hare   You might just as well say that "I like what I get" is the same thing as "I get what I like!"

The Dormouse   You might just as well say that "I breathe when I sleep" is the same thing as "I sleep when I breathe!"

If you go to a math conference you will be amazed. Everyone seems to understand each other perfectly well even though they use complex and intimidating symbols to communicate. Disputes seem to be confined to whether or not a mathematical proof works; rarely is it about the *language* of mathematics. That's because the symbolic nature of a mathematical proof insulates it from making any direct claims about reality. Albert Einstein wrote in his *Sidelights on Relativity* that "As far as the laws of mathematics refer to reality, they are not certain; and as far as they are certain, they do not refer to reality."

Definitions

Everyday language can be messy. Most words have multiple meanings, and sometimes even context doesn't help. Communication breaks down even in the best of circumstances (and it suffers compound fractures in politics). Luckily, logical analysis can help clarify some communication issues by revealing the commitments that underlie many ordinary statements. For example, one useful avenue into the workings of language is by way of definitions.

Logicians call the *meaning* of a term its *intension,* which is a list of the properties that the term *connotes* (its *sense*). For example, the term "clown" can be defined as having these properties: someone who wears silly costumes and zany makeup; a performer in a circus or theatrical setting; a person who performs slapstick routines or exhibits exaggerated and silly movements.

Knowing the meaning or sense of a term, and thinking outside the box, can help us in a variety of contexts, as illustrated in the following:

> A man is at the funeral of an old friend. He tentatively approaches the deceased's wife and asks whether he can say a word. The widow nods. The man clears his throat and says, "Plethora."
>
> The widow smiles appreciatively. "Thank you," she says. "That means a lot."

After all, he did ask whether he could say *a* word.

Logicians use the term *extension* to refer to the class members of a term, what the term *denotes* (its *reference*). The extension of the term "clown" includes Bozo, Clarabell, Homey the Clown, Mr. Noodle, Mr. Bean, and Krusty the Clown (feel free to add your favorite politician to the list). However, sometimes the reference of a term can be misunderstood in certain situations, as the following story illustrates:

> A middle-aged businessman is taking a taxi to the airport, and on the way he begins pontificating on the decline of morality among the younger generation. The businessman says to the taxi driver, "You

seem to be about my age. We certainly had more moral fiber than these kids today. For example, I didn't sleep with my wife before we were married. How about you?"

"I don't know," replies the taxi driver. "What is your wife's maiden name?"

When the businessman used the term "my wife," the extension was to one person, the businessman's wife. However, he (and everyone reading the story) expects his question to be interpreted as referring to "the taxi driver's wife." The humor results from the taxi driver's unexpected interpretation of the question as referring to the businessman's wife (as if the *extension* of the term "wife" had only one member as its reference).

The next story shows how a student tried to use the concept of reference in order to defuse his teacher's insinuation:

> A teacher questions her student: "You know, Mark, your essay about your dog Spot is identical to the one that your older sister handed in to me last year. How do you explain that?"
>
> "Oh, that's easy," says Mark. "It's the same dog."

Since Mark's essay was identical to his sister's essay, the teacher wanted Mark to confess to an act of plagiarism. The teacher assumed that the only explanation for the two essays being identical was that Mark copied his sister's essay. Mark's explanation instead focused on a different assumption: since the two essays referred to the same dog, the resulting essays were inevitably identical.

Many ordinary terms have intension (sense), but no extension (reference). For example, the term "Minotaur" can be defined as having the following properties: In Greek mythology, the Minotaur was a creature with the head of a bull on the body of a man. The term "Minotaur" has no extension; it denotes an empty class (a class without members). Other commonly used terms that some people believe have no extension are "honest politician," and "Santa Claus."

The commonly understood extension of a term can be used to take us to an unexpected place, as illustrated by the following conversation:

A parent says to her son, "How was school today?"
  The son replies, "We played a guessing game."
The parent says, "But I thought you had a math exam?"
  The boy says, "That's what I mean."

The fact that most terms have multiple definitions plays an important part in logic and in humor. Therefore, a novel way of defining a term can be insightful, as the following example illustrates.

For the final exam in an introduction to philosophy class the instructor assigned only one question: "What is courage?"
  A clever student wrote, "This" and turned it in.

Definitions can also help us understand what some mysterious fields of study are all about. For most people, philosophy and philosophers are strange objects that frighten even the best prepared students. The next time someone asks you what you do, tell them you are a philosophy professor and watch them panic. It's as if they think you are going to ask them an impossible question or engage you in some convoluted dialogue. Here's a nice definition of "philosopher" that Bertrand Russell offered in his book *The Problems of Philosophy*:

Whoever wishes to become a philosopher must learn not to be frightened by absurdities.

Russell's suggestion is particularly relevant to our discussion. Many jokes and humorous stories rely on absurd situations which are readily accepted as being necessary for the humor to work. But absurdities can be frightening in other situations, especially when we think it threatens our deeply held and cherished moral, religious, or political beliefs. Perhaps humor offers a way to teach us not to be frightened by the absurdities of life, or simply with situations that go awry. Since jokes and humor are merely fictional storytelling, the absurdities and breaches of patterns we normally rely on are not physically threatening to us. Perhaps they serve the purpose of teaching us to expect failures in the future, where things will not always go as we predict. Recognizing the absurd situation in a joke is a non-life-threatening experience that prepares our minds for the inevitable unpredictability and uncertainties of life.

People often define themselves by their political affiliations, religious beliefs, careers, professional associations, where they come from, and even by what they drive and own. But some people reject the customs and beliefs of their families and search for a new identity.

> A young person searched for a belief system he could wholeheartedly endorse. He almost became an atheist, but at the last minute he couldn't accept it. When asked why, he said, "I looked into it—they don't have any holidays."

Words and phrases can trip us up in countless ways. In the sentence, "He went down to the bank," the word "bank" might refer to a place where one deposits money, or it could refer to the side of a river. The context in which the sentence occurs will often clear up the matter, but there are exceptions:

> A tourist decided to take a walk in the countryside. When he unexpectedly came to a river, he noticed someone fishing on the opposite bank. The tourist yelled across, "Hello there—how can I get to the other side?"
>
> The fisherman looked up and down the river, thought for awhile and said, "You already are on the other side."

Although we understand that the reference of a term might be relative to a certain position (for example, "right" and "left"), we are still amused by the fisherman's unexpected response.

Communication confusion can sometimes result from a slang term being used whose new meaning is unknown to one of the parties. For instance, my son was trying on a pair of pants in a store dressing room and he yelled out, "These pants are *tight!*" Hearing this, I told him that I would get the next larger size to try on. He laughed and said, "Sorry, dad, the pants are perfect. I should have said 'These pants are *cool,*' then you would have understood me."

Here is another example where the uninitiated can be out of touch:

A new inmate is having his first dinner in the prison's cafeteria. A prisoner gets up and yells "17" and everyone in the cafeteria starts laughing hysterically. After a few minutes of quiet eating another prisoner gets up and says "65" and once again the crowd laughs heartily.

The new inmate is puzzled, so he asks the person next to him what was going on. He is told that the inmates have heard the same jokes for so many years that they have given the jokes numbers in order to save time. The new inmate gets up and yells "42" but the crowd remains stone cold silent. He asks the person next to him what happened.

"Some people just aren't good at telling jokes."

It's pretty bad when you can't even tell a number right. But the story points out another agreed upon definition—if people don't laugh when you tell a joke, then maybe you aren't a comedian.

Of course, communication can go haywire for any number of reasons:

A grasshopper walks into a bar and the bartender says to him, "Hey, guess what? We have a drink named after you."

The grasshopper looks surprised and says, "Wow, I can't believe it. You really have a drink named Raymond?"

The humor hinges on the fact that the term "you" usually refers to your identity, which is what the grasshopper assumed, so he was thrilled that a drink was named after him. Who wouldn't be?

The word "mouse" has several meanings. The most modern meaning, which began among computer users, is "a device to move the cursor across the screen of a monitor." What started out as a term used by a small number of computer users has turned into a term used by millions of people worldwide. Given the ubiquitous use of the term, the statement, "If you are going to the mall, then get me a new mouse. My old one died, and I need to finish my term paper this weekend," would probably not result in someone buying you a small rodent.

Science and mathematics are disciplines where precise definitions are necessary for providing technical meanings to special terms. The precise and unambiguous nature of technical definitions is used to reduce vagueness and to facilitate understanding. The following story shows how this process works:

An engineer and a mathematician are shown an area containing a herd of cows, and are asked to design an enclosure that will place the cows inside the smallest possible amount of fencing.

The engineer explains his design first: "I would design a circular fence. I would start with a large radius around the cows, and then pull the fence tight around the cows, because this will produce the smallest possible circular fence surrounding the cows."

The mathematician explains her design: "It's really quite simple. I would put a small circular fence around myself. I then define myself to be on the outside and the cows to be on the inside."

There are times when having a basic knowledge of the correct definition of a technical term would pay huge dividends:

A game show contestant is asked a science question: "If you are in a vacuum and someone calls your name, will you be able to hear it?"

The contestant looks puzzled, and then asks, "Is it on or off?"

As illustrated by the above story, in many cases it can help to know what objects are being referred to when we communicate with each other. We often learn about the extension of a term by having someone point to an object and attach a word to it. This process is called an *ostensive definition*. The process shows what an object looks like, but it does not provide synonyms or redefine the term by giving alternate meanings the way a dictionary definition does. In other words, it provides information regarding the extension (reference), but not the intension (sense) of a term. However, sometimes even seeing isn't believing:

Two college students go to Hawaii for spring break, and are lying on the beach at Waikiki working on their tans. One of them looks up and asks the other, "So which one do you think is farther away—Los Angeles or the Sun?"

The other one replies sarcastically, "Can you see Los Angeles?"

Another way to learn the meaning of a term is by a *functional definition* which describes the normal purpose (function) of the items associated with the term. For example, a functional definition of a "door stopper" might be "a device used to prevent a door from closing." This functional definition allows a door stopper to be made of almost any kind of material, as long as it fulfills the purpose in mind. It can be metal, plastic, or rubber. You can even fold some paper and jam it under the door, or you can stack some books against the door.

Most manufactured objects have been created and designed for specific purposes or functions. However, on the TV program *MacGyver*, the main character solves problems by using objects out of their typical domain. He uses everyday objects to solve novel problems for which the object was not originally intended. In doing so, MacGyver extends the functional definitions of the objects.

Of course, a functional definition does not tell you what an object looks like. The complementary nature of ostensive and functional definitions can be illustrated by considering two questions. First, an appropriate response to the question, "What is that thing?" can be provided by giving an ostensive definition, for example, "That's an alternator." Second, an appropriate response to the question, "What does that thing do?" can be provided by giving a functional definition, for example, "An alternator charges your car battery and provides some power to your car's electrical systems." Here's an interesting example:

> After a late evening out, a college student is showing her apartment to
> a new acquaintance. He notices a large bass drum in the corner.
>   "Oh, do you play the drums?"
> "No, that's my new clock."
>   "That can't be a clock."
> "Sure it can. Watch this." She then begins drumming loudly. A neighbor
> yells out, "Stop that pounding! It's two o'clock in the morning!"

On the other hand, sometimes ostensive definitions need some help, too:

A father is proudly showing his daughter the ocean for the first time. The daughter stares at the vast expanse and says, "Look at all that water, Dad!"

"Yes, and that's only the top!"

Finally, knowing how companies measure or define things can help us make smart consumer choices:

A customer asks a waiter, "How much does one hard-boiled egg cost?"
"That'll be $1."
"How much do two hard-boiled eggs cost?"
"$1.50"
"Okay, I'll have the second egg, then."

You Left Out The Best Part

Normal everyday communication uses shorthand. This is especially true if the people conversing share a lot of background experience. In those instances, it is not necessary to spell out every detail about a situation, because each party is confident that the other will fill in the missing parts. If any misunderstanding does occur, then the on-going nature of the communication allows for clarification. That is, unless the two people involved in the conversation have been together too long:

An elderly couple has been living together for 50 years, but they were never married. One day, Shirley says, "You know, Benny, I was thinking that maybe we should get married."

Benny thinks for a while and says, "Nah, who would have us?"

Once again, we see how humor can result from the unexpected interpretation of a key term or phrase. When we read the story we naturally interpret the phrase "we should get married" to mean that the two persons in the story should marry *each other*. Our expectation fuels the humor by upending what we normally expect.

In many cases, filling in the missing parts is quite easy. For example, suppose someone meets a friend on the street and says the following:

> Look what I just bought. It's the new album, "Your Head Is Screwed on Wrong," by The Exiled Physicians. I know I'm going to love it.

The speaker assumes that the friend will supply the purposely left out missing information:

> Look what I just bought. It's the new album, "Your Head Is Screwed on Wrong," by The Exiled Physicians. *I loved all the other albums by that group, so* I know I'm going to love it.

Logicians refer to an argument with a missing premise or a missing conclusion as an *enthymeme*. (Since you asked, the term is a combination of "*en*" which means "in," and "*thymos*" which refers to "a part of the mind." Quite simply, the term means "in the mind." Therefore, any missing information is *implied* by the speaker or writer.) Since arguments of this kind leave out important information, they rely on context for their understanding. Most writers and public speakers don't want to bore their audiences with every fine detail, so they purposely leave out details which they assume will be filled in easily. Of course, there are times when we might not be familiar with the missing information. For example, someone might say this at a party:

> I drive a Porsche 918 Spyder, so maintenance is not a problem.

Many people don't even know what one of those cars look like, let alone how much it costs, but the speaker won't know that unless you open your mouth to ask. Instead, the speaker has assumed something like the following:

> I drive a Porsche 918 Spyder, *and as anyone who owns one knows, they require very little upkeep,* so maintenance is not a problem.

Ad agencies are given enormous sums of money to come up with catchy slogans and slick commercials to sell products. In the early days of television, commercials lasted a long time. The manufacturers had the spokesperson point out in great detail the wonderful features and functionality of the product. Today's commercials are very different. They often last no more than a few seconds, and some don't even have any spoken words. The ads are often effective because they know consumers will fill in missing information. For example, a commercial might show a group of attractive young people having fun at a beach party. The ad will make sure to showcase the clothes being worn, and it might end with these words on the screen:

Our clothes make all the difference.

In this fictional commercial the advertisers are smart enough to know that their target audience will unconsciously fill in the missing information. What will happen is that in the minds of many of the viewers there will be a finished argument: "*I want to be part of that group having fun. Wearing that company's clothes will make all the difference, so I better buy some of their clothes.*" The addition of catchy and popular music and glossy videos can be powerful forces behind implied argumentation. But does this kind of stuff work? Check your mind the next time you look at one of those ads (or check your clothes closet).

Some clever enthymemes put a twist on the meaning of words and incorporate multiple logical aspects into the mix:

A train station is a place where trains stop. A bus station is a place where buses stop. On my desk there is a work station.

The joke uses the force of an enthymeme to get us to actively fill in the missing conclusion, by playing with the words *station* and *stop*. The simplicity of the three statements masks the complex underlying logical structures, so when we unpack it and solve the puzzle we are delighted at being tricked.

Rhetorical Language

Arguments don't occur in a vacuum (regardless of whether the vacuum is on or off). They rely on context for an appreciation and correct analysis.

All too often, what people say or write is ripped out of context and given a bogus interpretation. That is why we should always seek the original setting for a complete view of the reasoning involved. Knowledge of the setting, the people, and the topics helps to expose inaccuracies of interpretation. However, sometimes language is used purposely in a non-literal manner, often for exaggeration or sarcasm or effect.

Rhetorical questions are meant to be statements. They are used extensively by both prosecutors and defense attorneys to get a witness to assert for the court, under oath, something that the attorney is supposed to already know. But some questions are better left unasked, and there are times when we go too far, when our speaking outruns our common sense. The absurdity is sometimes missed by us (if everyone but you is laughing, then you missed it). Clarence Darrow told the following story about his early days as a trial lawyer:

> If I have any advice to give to young lawyers it is this: Don't ask too many questions of a witness. Just get them to say what you want, and then stop. I learned this lesson the hard way. I was defending a client who was accused of biting off the ear of someone in a bar fight. I asked a witness, "Did you see my client bite off the ear?" The witness said, "No, I didn't." At this point I should have dismissed the witness. But being young and naïve I asked one more question: "Well then, how can you be sure that my client bit off the ear?" The witness said, "Because I saw him spit it out."

A double moral lesson to be learned from Darrow's story—one for lawyers, and one for their clients: There are times when it's better to keep your mouth shut.

There are many ways to construct an argument. We can use straightforward statements, or we can misdirect by asserting something in the form of a question. For example, a parent may say this to a teenager still living at home.

> After you graduate from college you will need to look for a full-time job. You will have to consider a career. Suppose you get a job interacting

with the public. Do you think that most employers will hire you if have tattoos all over your face?

The final sentence is a question, but it is certainly meant rhetorically. The parent has one and only one answer in mind, so it is really an assertion. But the teenager can completely disagree with the parent's intended assertion. He can use the question as a springboard to enlighten the parent about the numerous job possibilities where facial tattoos will not be factor. And if that doesn't work, he can always ask (rhetorically) the question, "Do you really think I want to grow up to be just like you?"

Of course not all questions are rhetorical, nor do they always miss the mark. We sometimes ask questions simply to get new information, or to get directions, or to get to know someone better, and for lots of other reasons. Of course, some of the answers we receive may be quite unexpected:

Professor   What inspired you to write this essay?

Student   The due date.

Students are subjected to multiple-choice, problem-solving, and essay questions. Final exams are often comprehensive and are meant to test what students have learned from a course. Capturing the essence of a course succinctly is a challenge for even the brightest students:

For a final exam in a logic class the professor writes on the blackboard the following sentence: "Is this a question?"

Most students are stumped. Some write furiously, adding anything that they remembered from the class.

But one confident student writes a single sentence, hands it to the teacher, and smiles as she leaves. She wrote: "If that is a question, then this is an answer."

Now that's a clever use of language. If that student doesn't deserve to get an A+, then no one does. Although the joke and the student's answer depend on an understanding of the logical underpinnings of language, its humorous impact is immediate.

The Portrait Puzzle

Two people are looking at a portrait of a young girl. One person introduces himself as Shane and asks the other if she knows the identity of the person in the portrait. Carly responds mysteriously as follows: "I have no sisters or brothers, but the mother of the young girl in the portrait is my mother's daughter."

Assuming that Carly is telling the truth, who is in the portrait?

4

Origin Of The Specious

Whenever we think, perceive, form judgments, act, or calculate, we are using our *cognitive* abilities. Although these mental abilities are directly involved in our conscious decisions and logical reasoning, we are also subject to many unconscious psychological factors that often interfere with our mental abilities. The *unconscious factors* that can *negatively* impact how we process and interpret information, how we make judgments and decisions, and how we create and evaluate arguments, are called *cognitive biases*.

One of the reasons why humans were able to survive as a species is our ability to observe what is happening around us and to use that information to make *fast* judgments. This is certainly not unique to humans; successful organisms of all kinds have the ability to react quickly to their environments. Although these abilities are triggered by specific sensations or perceptions, they are not always necessary for survival. For example, a perception of sudden motion around us, or a loud sound, or a large object moving toward us may cause us to run or shield ourselves from *possible* danger. Although it is also possible that no danger actually exists, the ability to react quickly to different kinds of events is crucial because often there is no time to carefully assess a situation. However, as we shall see, some of those innate quick survival abilities can *interfere* with our equally important ability to carry out long deliberations, to make careful judgments and decisions, and to assess the strength of arguments.

Heuristics and Algorithms

Situations that do not require quick decision-making give us the time to think about possible outcomes, thus allowing us to draw on personal experience. When we have time to deliberate, it is natural to rely on *heuristics*, sometimes referred to as good old *common sense* (however, some critics have stressed that "common sense" is neither common nor sensible). Heuristics rely on the assumption that the future will resemble the past. We justify the use of a heuristic when we say our decision is based on an "educated guess," one that is backed up by knowledge and experience. However, since a *decision* is based on a *judgment*, and since judgments are often the result of *cognitive biases*, some of our decisions *may* be negatively impacted by those biases. The following is an example where learning from the past should help when giving advice.

> When Lucy was about to paint her apartment, she recalled seeing her neighbor paint his apartment a few months before. Since their apartments were the same size, Lucy asked Mack, "How many gallons of paint did you buy when you painted your apartment?"
> "I bought eight gallons," said Mack.
> Lucy bought eight gallons and began painting. She finished the entire apartment but she had to use only four gallons of paint. Puzzled by this, she went to see Mack.
> "I bought eight gallons of paint, but I was able to paint my entire apartment with only four gallons," said Lucy.
> Mack said, "Oh, so that happened to you, too!"

Mack obviously didn't trust his own experience as being good evidence for future results. The next time she asks Mack for advice, let's hope Lucy remembers what happened.

Heuristics are shortcuts (*rules of thumb*) that we use to make decisions. Although relying on these mental shortcuts shortens the time needed to make a decision, they cannot guarantee a successful outcome. For example, if a detective trying to solve a murder notices that nothing was stolen from the victim, she might judge that it was not a crime of gain. By using the preliminary evidence to conjecture that it might be a crime of passion, the detective's decision illustrates the use of a heuristic to help begin identifying potential suspects. This process may or may not lead to the solution of the crime. We need to recognize that the strengths of heuristics are that they simplify decision-making and are often reliable; but the weaknesses are that they can lead to bias and incorrect judgments.

An *algorithm* is a step-by-step procedure that ensures a consistent starting point and end point. We hear a lot about how algorithms are used to gather information about people who use electronic devices. The complex programs (also called *engines*) are able to track our every move as we bounce from one website to another, social media platform, phone app, or simply through our GPS systems. The algorithms analyze the data about us so companies can not only try to predict our future behavior, they can also try to affect our beliefs.

On the other hand, an algorithm can be as simple as a cooking recipe, offering you a step-by-step procedure to prepare a meal. Here's an example from a fictional *Thief's Guide to One-Pot Meals*:

> First, steal two chickens. Next, surreptitiously gather some vegetables
> from your neighbor's garden. Boil some water. Add ingredients, bring
> to a boil again, then reduce the heat and simmer for one hour. Enjoy it
> until they catch you.

But even the simplest recipe algorithm can prove to be too difficult for some people, as the next example illustrates:

> Two college students are discussing how hard it is having their own
> apartment and being responsible for taking care of themselves.
> "Take cooking," one of them says. "It's way too hard. Every single
> recipe starts out the same: Use a clean bowl."

Both heuristics and algorithms are used to solve everyday problems. For example, depending on their levels of experience and training, two auto mechanics might use *different heuristic* procedures to attack a problem. Since they apply different procedures, they might have different outcomes. On the other hand, a large automotive company may have access to expensive and sophisticated electronic diagnostic machines. These machines connect to a car's computer system, and they follow the same *algorithm* each time, so each problem is efficiently diagnosed by the same series of steps.

When you try to find a lost item in your house, you generally start looking for it in the last place you recall seeing it. This simple strategy is a heuristic, and its success depends on a number of factors, such as how sure you are that your memory is correct, or whether someone else moved the item since you last saw it. See if you can spot the kind of procedure used in this next example from everyday life.

> A police officer sees someone crawling on the ground under a street light, so she decides to investigate. The person says that he is looking for his lost car keys. After searching for a few minutes the officer asks the man if he is sure that this is where the keys were lost. The man says, "No, it was down the block a little ways, but there's more light over here."

Heuristics and Cognitive Biases

Early investigations into the connection between heuristics and cognitive biases focused either on calculations that involved probability assessments, or rules of logic. The results of these early experiments indicated that most people make simple mistakes that could be explained as stemming from the unconscious reliance on cognitive biases. Here is an example:

> You are told that a candy bar and a bottle of soda together cost $1.10. (This ridiculously small sum proves that the example is purely fictional). You are also told that the bottle of soda costs $1 more than the candy bar. Assuming that this information is correct, you are then asked to calculate how much the candy bar costs.

Most people say that the candy bar costs ten cents. If that is your answer, then sorry, you are wrong. Here's why: If the candy bar costs ten cents, then according to the problem, the bottle of soda would cost *one dollar more*, meaning that the bottle of soda costs $1.10. If so, together the two items would cost $1.20. The correct answer is the candy bar costs five cents, and the bottle of soda costs *one dollar more*, so it costs $1.05. Together they cost $1.10.

Research suggests that people who get the wrong answer most likely make a quick assessment of the problem, so they *unconsciously* simplify the problem by judging it to be the sum of two figures: $1 and ten cents. This unconscious heuristic results in the incorrect answer. Research continues to look for links between the human reliance on heuristics and cognitive biases that can seriously impact our judgments and decisions.

We react to the world in several ways. Our brains, nervous systems, and muscles have evolved to automatically respond to specific stimuli. For example, if you try to catch a falling object, you don't *consciously* calculate the object's motion, nor do you have to think about what muscles to move. This kind of function is part of what is called the automatic *intuitive* judgment system. In contrast, decisions that allow us more time to deliberate fall under the self-aware *reflective* system. For example, we might spend a considerable amount of time deciding what kind of car to buy, considering along the way the car's price, possible financing, insurance, registration, gas mileage, and upkeep.

Confirmation Bias

Everyone has certain beliefs they feel justified in holding. However, research indicates that many of our beliefs get reinforced by a cognitive process that selectively screens out or minimizes the importance of evidence that undermines those beliefs. This psychological factor is called *confirmation bias*. The bias can lead us to dismiss opposing viewpoints without any careful consideration or logical assessment. The bias also manifests itself in the types of information we seek out. Although the internet offers the chance to explore different sides of a question, many of us search only for information that agrees with our settled beliefs. Since this results in our returning to the same sources of information, our political and social positions remain unchallenged.

Research shows that when subjects are given evidence that *supports* their belief, along with evidence that *goes against* their belief, the subjects show a strong tendency to not only recall more of the supportive evidence, but also to rank it as more credible. The following illustrates how confirmation bias can affect judgments.

Customer service representative   "How may I help you?"

Customer   "I bought a three-month supply of your pills. Your advertisement stated that they would make me smarter. But now I want my money back because they don't work. I think you cheated me."

Customer service representative   "See, they're working already!"

Status Quo Bias

It is certainly reasonable to rely on past experience to make decisions. Moreover, when we need to make a quick decision, some ideas will obviously come to mind before others. However, this unconscious process is the basis for the *status quo bias,* the tendency to react the same way each time just because the idea or notion came quickly to mind. Unfortunately, this means that the status quo bias can also stop us from making a change that would be beneficial.

It is not easy for us to make substantial changes in our lives. For example, some people remain in a relationship that is not satisfying, even though they know they should end it. This might happen because of the *uncertainly* attached to any substantial change. The bias can also affect other situations such as career changes. It can reveal itself in politics when voters continue to support an elected official in the face of serious shortcomings simply because of the uncertainty involved in voting for someone else. There is an old saying that captures the psychological underpinning of the status quo bias: "Better the devil you know than the devil you don't know." It does seem that much of today's political discourse involves people who firmly adhere to that saying. Luckily, there is a joke that cuts through this:

Zeke   "What kind of fool do you take me for?"

Bailey   "Is there more than one kind?"

The status quo bias contributes to our tendency to want to keep things the same. It rests on the psychological fear of the unknown simply because it is unknown.

Functional Fixedness Bias

The psychologist, Abraham Maslow, wrote the following in his book *The Psychology of Science*: "I suppose it is tempting, if the only tool you have is a hammer, to treat everything as if it were a nail." The tendency to see objects as having only one use is called *functional fixedness bias*, and it results in a closed mind about the function of an object. A more flexible attitude about *possible* functions might enable us to use something out of its normal range. For example, if you need to drink some water but don't have a cup handy, then you can cup your hands together to hold the water. When we break out of the "fixed" perception of an object we are *thinking outside the box.*

The functional fixedness bias is also involved in a narrow judgment of someone's potential ability. For example, parents who push their child into a particular career path might fail to recognize that the child has a desire to explore a path that is not valued by the parents.

Similarly, an owner of a company might fail to see that a worker who is competent in one job could also prove valuable in a different position within a company, thus restricting the worker's possibility of advancement.

My boss arrived at work in a brand-new Lamborghini. "Wow, that's an amazing car," I said. My boss replied, "Yes it is. And if you work hard, put in extra hours, and strive for excellence, then I'll be able to get another one next year."

Ingroup Bias

The tendency to ascribe positive stereotypes to the members of our ingroup, and negative stereotypes to members of outgroups is called the *ingroup bias.* This psychological factor can generate an unwarranted fear and suspicion of the members of outgroups. It can also contribute to an unwarranted judgment of superiority to the members of the ingroup. The ingroup bias deflects evidence that goes against a mistaken stereotype, as illustrated by the saying "The exception proves the rule." The psychological processes at play here are similar to the confirmation bias, but the ingroup bias has a very narrow focus.

> A television news reporter interviews a person on the street. The reporter says, "There is an important election in two months. However, a large number of people seem not to be paying attention to the issues. Can you tell me what you believe is causing such *ignorance* and *apathy* among that group?"
> The person responds, "I don't know, and I don't care."

Fundamental Attribution Bias

The psychological factor that leads us to *regard* someone's behavior as stemming from that person's basic character or personality traits, and to *disregard* the role of situational or environmental forces is called the *fundamental attribution bias.* This occurs when we automatically judge that someone's mistakes or failures are the result of their personality flaws. This tendency can lead to many serious, dangerous, and unwarranted judgments. For example, someone might claim that the perpetrator of a crime has certain personality flaws that led to the commission of the crime. But that same person might also blame the victim, as if the victim had it coming because of their own personality flaws.

In contrast, we have a tendency to *excuse* our mistakes and flaws as stemming from outside forces, not from our personality. In other words, our psychological biases cause us to "explain" other people's failures as being their fault, but "excuse" our failures as being not our fault.

> When a man opens the front door, a Census worker announces that she needs to get some information from the homeowner. The surly

man shouts, "Why are you wasting my time. I already sent in your ridiculous forms!"

"I'm sorry sir, but we haven't received them yet. Perhaps you can just answer a few simple questions. For example, what is your occupation?"

"I'm an engineer, not that it's any of your business. I don't have time to waste answering your useless questions, so buzz off!"

"So I take it you're not a *civil* engineer."

What Can We Do?

Although there is evidence to indicate that certain cognitive biases are hard-wired into us, there is also evidence that indicates we can sometimes overcome unconscious biases. For example, students who have learned basic statistical concepts, or who have knowledge of probability calculations, are less likely to make simple statistical or mathematical errors. This holds true for students who take logic and critical thinking courses. For example, since the Graduate Record Examination (GRE) and the Law School Admission Test (LSAT) have logical reasoning questions, logic and critical thinking students are well-prepared to handle the kinds of questions that require logical analysis. The training and experience allows us to slow down the automatic intuitive judgment system, so we can apply the deliberation skills available in our self-aware reflective system.

Cognitive biases not only hinder our ability to rationally interpret information, they can also contribute to fallacious reasoning. Arguments should provide premises that support a conclusion, but they can fall short for a variety of reasons, and some special instances of failure are called *fallacies*.

Informal fallacies are reasoning mistakes in everyday language that often go unnoticed. They occur for a variety of reasons, such as an intended or unintended change in the *meaning* of a term (the *intension*) or its *reference* (the *extension*). In fact, there are so many types of fallacious reasoning that the philosopher, Arthur Schopenhauer, wrote in his essay *The Art of Controversy*, "It would be a very good thing if every trick could receive some short and obviously appropriate name, so that when a man used this or that particular trick, he could be at once reproached for it." Schopenhauer would have been delighted to hear that dozens of fallacies have been identified and named.

Complex Question Fallacy

We can get into trouble if we respond incorrectly to a complex question, which occurs when a single question contains several hidden parts. Quite often the questioner tries to force a single answer that, in turn, can be used against the respondent. For example, suppose you are asked the following question: "Do you still rob banks?" If you answer either "yes" or "no," then you are admitting that you have robbed banks. If you can see that a complex question is two questions packed into one, then you can sidestep the trap. Hidden in the complex question above are two separate questions: (1) Did you ever rob banks? and (2) Do you now rob banks? Once these two questions are brought into the open then you can truthfully respond "No" to both questions and extricate yourself from the situation. (That is, unless you do rob banks.)

There are other benefits to breaking a question into multiple parts. The comedian Professor Irwin Corey, who was billed as *The World's Foremost Authority*, wore a tuxedo, a string tie, and black sneakers. He was once asked the question, "Why do you wear sneakers?" Here is the Professor's wonderful response:

> That's a two-part question. First you ask, "Why?" The question "Why?" has been plaguing mankind since time immemorial. Statesmen, philosophers, educators, and scientists have all been asking the crucial question, "Why?" And in these few moments allocated to me, it would be ludicrous on my part, for the sake of brevity, to delve into the ultimate "Why?"
>
> Now to the second part of your question: "Do I wear sneakers?" – *Yes!*

Circular Reasoning Fallacy

Circular reasoning occurs when information that is initially presented is then used as justification for itself. The next story illustrates this process:

> Vinnie is visited by an auditor from the IRS. The auditor says, "According to our records, you live in a 20,000 sq. ft. house with 15 bedrooms and 12 bathrooms, situated on 300 acres of land. In addition, you have a Rolls-Royce, a Bentley, a Lamborghini, and three Ferraris. You also own a string of racehorses. However, for the last ten years you stated on your tax returns that you have no annual income."
>
> Vinnie replies that everything the IRS auditor had said was correct. "Well then," says the IRS auditor, "there's a big problem. How can you explain your lavish lifestyle with no income?"
>
> "Oh, that's simple," says Vinnie. "About ten years ago I discovered an old treasure chest full of gold and jewels, so that explains my huge wealth."
>
> The IRS auditor looks skeptical and asks, "Can you prove your story?"
>
> "Of course," replies Vinnie. "Look around. I own a 20,000 sq. ft. house with 15 bedrooms and 12 bathrooms . . ."

Vinnie tries to convince the auditor by using the following strategy:

Argument 1
Premise: I discovered an old treasure chest full of gold and jewels.
Conclusion: I am very wealthy.

The auditor then questions the premise and asks for proof that Vinnie discovered an old treasure chest full of gold and jewels. Vinnie's "proof" is this:

Argument 2
Premise: I am very wealthy.
Conclusion: I discovered an old treasure chest full of gold and jewels.

Vinnie simply switches the order of the premise and conclusion of the first argument as his so-called proof. The two arguments display the circular reasoning fallacy.

Hasty Generalization Fallacy

In our zeal to make sense of the world, we often jump the gun and make judgments which go far beyond the limited information available. How often have you heard someone quickly stereotype an entire group of people based on one bad experience with a member of that particular group? A little reflection on the matter reveals the improbability that such a small sample could truly represent an entire group of people. For example, suppose you traveled to a foreign country and during your stay you encountered only two people who spoke English. You might conclude that a tiny percentage of the people in that country speak English. However, your conclusion would be unjustified because your small sample is unlikely to be representative of millions of citizens of that country. Hasty generalizations like these are made on the basis of *limited personal experience*. The psychological factor that can lead us to make incorrect generalizations, judgments and arguments is called the *availability bias*.

An argument whose conclusion about a large group is based solely on a few personal experiences is called the *hasty generalization fallacy*. This type of argument is generally quite weak. Of course, a hasty generalization can be a great source of humor:

I told my psychiatrist that everyone hates me. He said I was being ridiculous. After all, everyone hasn't met me yet.

There are many instances where we overstep the bounds of reason, and if we just think about what we are about to say before we open our mouths, we could avoid embarrassing ourselves. For instance, suppose someone says,

All generalizations are false.

If you hear that, your response should be "I think what you said is true." That should keep the person busy for a while. On the other hand, suppose a second person says this:

No one makes generalizations anymore.

In that case, tell them to go talk to the first person. They should have a good time going around in circles.

False Dichotomy Fallacy

Another interesting fallacy is the *false dichotomy*; it occurs when it is assumed that only two choices are possible for a given situation, when in fact other choices obviously exist. Examples of these kinds of fallacies are not hard to locate. You can encounter them by turning on any TV program that showcases the interaction between two political polar opposites as they hurl schoolyard insults at each other. Sooner or later, someone is bound to says the following:

You have to agree with me, or else you are a fool.

The verbal challenge offers two alternatives, but it doesn't require a Mensa genius to realize that there are more than two possibilities. Here is one possibility: "I can agree with you, or I'm a fool, or my position is correct." But perhaps the simplest way of dealing with this situation is to say, "If I have to agree with you, then I really am a fool."

Ad Hominem Fallacy

People often try to smuggle irrelevant information to support a conclusion. To add insult to injury, these same people often rely on psychological or emotional appeals for their persuasive force. We should apply rational and objective means to determine both the truth of a statement and the strength of an argument. When we reject someone's argument simply on the basis of an alleged "character flaw" of the person, then we are committing an *ad hominem fallacy* (literally, "against the person"). In most cases, a person's character is irrelevant to the truth or falsity of their assertion. (A relevant exception is when a person has been exposed as a congenital liar.)

Clear cases of ad hominem are not usually hard to spot, but clever ones know how to push people's emotional buttons. A common form of this is when someone's argument is attacked by way of a negative stereotype. The following is a good example:

> **Joe**   I happen to know Micah, and I can safely say that he doesn't know the meaning of the word *fear*.
>
> **Mary**   I know Micah as well as you do, and I can safely say that he doesn't know the meaning of a lot of words.

Equivocation Fallacy

The *equivocation* fallacy involves an ambiguity that occurs when a word or phrase shifts meaning (intentionally or unintentionally). This can easily happen because many words and phrases have several different meanings. Here is an example of someone intentionally shifting the meaning of a seemingly straightforward phrase:

> Stephanie was awakened by a loud knock on the front door. An obviously irritated man identified himself as a bill collector. He said, "I'm here to find out why you have failed to make any payments on the new furnace we installed."
>
> Stephanie wiped the sleep from her eyes and yawned, "When your salespeople came and talked me into getting a new furnace, they told me it would pay for itself in less than a year."

Stephanie bought the furnace because she was intrigued by the prospect that it would "pay for itself." Imagine her surprise when she was told that the furnace hasn't yet sent in any payments.

An instance of equivocation can have serious effects—but luckily it can also lead to humorous results. Here is a good example:

My husband and I were famished after hours of driving nonstop, so we pulled over at a truck stop. While he gassed up the car, I went into the restaurant and placed a large order to go. After writing it all down, the person behind the register asked, "Will that be all for you?"

"No," I replied, "Some of it is for my husband."

The term "all" has two distinct meanings in the passage. The counterperson is asking the customer *if that is the entire order*. The customer interprets the counterperson as asking the customer *if the order was for her alone*.

Equivocation usually happens very quickly. In some cases of humor, the swift, unexpected change in the meaning of a key word or phrase is essential to carry the joke while it pleasantly jars our minds. In fact, for many jokes the faster the better, as illustrated by the following:

The teacher said to the class, "I wish you'd pay a little attention."
One student replied, "We're paying as little attention as we can."

The philosopher-logician-mathematician-magician-musician Raymond Smullyan (yes, that's right, he was an expert in all those fields) once remarked, "I'd give my right arm to be ambidextrous."

The world of sports offers some fine examples of how multiple meanings of a term can lead to unexpected and humorous results. The first one was intentional, but the second surely wasn't.

After his team was badly defeated in a game, a football coach was asked what he thought of his team's execution. "I'm all for it," said the coach.

*   *   *

A baseball manager was asked about his star player returning to the team after having gone through a drug rehabilitation program. "It's a real shot in the arm for the team," he replied.

Even Mahatma Gandhi was able to use an unexpected shift in the meaning of a term to form a clever response. When Gandhi was asked what he thought of Western civilization, he replied "I think that it would be a good idea."

Composition Fallacy

Some statements take a legitimate characteristic of the individual parts of an object and erroneously transfer it to the entire object. For example, suppose someone said the following about a Sumo wrestler:

> Every cell in his body is tiny, so he must be tiny.

In this example of the *composition fallacy*, a true characteristic of the cells of a person is mistakenly applied to the size of the entire person. Composition fallacies can even occur when the outcome of a situation is not yet known, as shown in the following prediction:

> Each of the ingredients you are using to bake the cake tastes delicious. Thus, the cake will taste delicious.

The conclusion might turn out to be false, especially if the person doesn't know how to use an oven correctly (the cake is under- or over-cooked). Also, sometimes even the best-tasting and best-smelling ingredients do not mesh with each other.

However, not every argument that proceeds from the individual parts of an object is fallacious. For example, "Every thread of these pants is blue; thus, the pants are blue," is a perfectly reasonable result. But the same can't be said of the next case:

> A lawyer defending a man accused of burglary tried this creative defense: "My client merely inserted his arm into the window and removed a few small items from the house. It should be painfully obvious to everyone, your honor, that his arm is not him. Therefore, I fail to see how you can punish the entire man for an offense committed by his arm."
>
> "That was well argued," the judge replied. "Therefore, using your reasoning, I sentence the defendant's arm to one year in prison. He can accompany his arm or not, as he chooses."

Ouch. This is a clear-cut case where failing to see the possible consequences of an argument can jump up and bite you if you are not careful. Perhaps it's simply that some lawyers are too clever for their own good.

Division Fallacy

The *division fallacy* occurs when a characteristic of an object taken as a whole is erroneously transferred to the individual parts (this is the opposite of the composition fallacy). For example, suppose someone said this of our Sumo wrestler:

> He is fantastically large, so all of his cells must be large.

For reasons similar to the composition fallacy, we must be on guard not to rush to judgment. After all, not every argument that proceeds from the whole object to the individual parts is fallacious. For example, "That is a metal desk, so the top is made of metal," is acceptable reasoning.

Curious cases of fallacies can break out at any time. Here is an example how fallacious reasoning can make a weak argument seem like it has some sense to it.

> "Wake up," said George to his wife. "The baby is crying and he needs feeding."
>
> Martha responded, "Well, you feed him, he's your son." George replied, "But he's half yours."
>
> "Of course," said Martha. "But it's your half that's crying."

Gambler's Fallacy

Many people have heard of the *gambler's fallacy*. There are actually quite a few variations on the main theme which has to do with a misunderstanding of probabilities. Most games of chance in casinos are purposely designed to offer gamblers poor odds. (Las Vegas casinos don't like the word "gambling," they prefer the innocuous sounding term "gaming." But a bad bet by any other name is still a bad bet.) For example, most roulette tables in the United States have 38 possible outcomes: 18 red numbers, 18 black numbers and two green numbers (0 and 00). If you bet a dollar on one of the 38 possibilities and it comes up, the casino will give you 35 dollars, and you get to keep your original dollar, for a total of 36 dollars. But a game with "true" odds would be one where you get a total of 38 dollars when you win. Of course, a game like that would mean that the casino would no longer have an edge. And that would mean the end of billion dollar casinos.

As all casino dealers will tell you, and what all mathematicians know, roulette tables have no memory. Whatever happens on one spin has no effect on the next. If red comes up, then red has the same probability of coming up the next spin, and the spin after that, and the spin after that. So, a gambler's fallacy occurs when someone thinks that because red came up three times in a row it is less likely to come up on the next spin. This erroneous thinking is a misapplication of the idea that over the course of millions of spins the color probabilities will approach their expected mathematical results (47.4% Red, 47.4% Black, and 5.2% Green). But the probabilities that will be reached after millions of spins have no bearing on any one spin or on any short run of spins.

The following story concerns horseracing, called *The Sport of Kings*, and it illustrates the typical life of a gambler—sorry, *gamer*:

> A man who had been betting on horses for over fifty years happened to be a contestant on a game show, and he was doing quite well. The game show host said, "Now, the final question is worth $100,000. Can you tell me who won the 1978 Kentucky Derby?"
>
> The contestant answered, "No, but I can tell you who came in fourth."

Professional gamblers get the joke immediately because they have been on the losing end of a bet numerous times. A "bad beat" occurs when a seemingly winning bet suddenly, unexpectedly, and cruelly turns into a losing bet. For example, your horse comes in first but is disqualified for an infraction such as bumping another horse. In the story above, the gambler knows who came in fourth because that's who he bet on. Losing bets are hard to forget.

Grammatical Confusion

Instances of ambiguity that arise from misuse of grammar are called *amphiboly* (yes, logicians like to use using Latin and Greek based terms). However, many of those instances often lead to unintentionally humorous results. This can occur because the mangled syntax of a statement muddles the intended meaning. Try to decipher this example:

> Sipping on cold coffee the corpse lay in front of the tired detective.

If the corpse is the one sipping on cold coffee, then the tired detective surely has a difficult case to solve.

Here are a few examples from the zany world of car insurance underwriting. The claimants tried their best to explain what happened, but wound up getting entangled in the web of grammar.

> I had been driving for 40 years when I feel asleep at the wheel and had an accident.

* * *

> I was thrown from my car as it left the road. I was later found in a ditch by some stray cows.

Moral Dilemmas

There are situations that seem to be similar to false dichotomies, but which have a distinctive character. Situations in which we are confronted with conflicting moral choices are called *moral dilemmas*. These occur when there are only two actions to chose from, and there are compelling moral reasons for each action, but we can choose to do only one. This puts us in a quandary, in that no matter which choice we make we seem doomed to moral failure by not having done the other action. Moral dilemmas are challenging because they put us in a no-win situation. The result is that any choice we make has unwanted consequences, a situation often referred to as being *between a rock and a hard place*. In these instances, someone might advise you to *choose the lesser of two evils*. Such sage advice might lead to an unexpected decision:

> If you are forced to choose between two evils, then you should choose the one you haven't tried yet.

The next example illustrates a typical *misapplication* of the concept:

> My rich uncle is going to buy me any car I want. But now I'm stuck with a terrible moral dilemma. Should I get a Lamborghini or a Ferrari?

We should all be so lucky. It is obvious that since neither choice will lead to an unsatisfactory end, this is not a moral dilemma. As usual, comedians have figured out a way to illustrate moral dilemmas that are as clear as they are clever. Here's a rather poignant one:

> An old woman had two chickens that she adored. However, one of the chickens got sick, so the woman made chicken soup out of the other one to help the sick one get well.

There are many stories about moral situations or conflicts that don't necessarily rise to the level of moral dilemmas, but are enlightening in other ways. Here is one about a tense family situation that was successfully defused by a wise judge:

> Two sisters argued about how to divide a large piece of land that they inherited. The older sister thought she deserved more, since she was the first born. But the younger sister said that she should get more since she will probably live longer and will need more income from the land.
>
> They went to a judge for help. "I'll toss a coin, and whoever calls it correctly gets to choose how big each piece of land will be," said the judge. Of course, each sister was afraid of losing because they both believed that the winner would divide up the land unequally. They told the judge of their concern.
>
> "That won't be a problem," replied the judge. "You see, the one who wins gets to divide the land, but the other one gets first choice."

Business ethics studies the moral responsibilities related to business actions and decisions. Here is a story that illustrates a moral conflict inherent in many profit-oriented enterprises:

A co-owner of a business was trying to explain to her young daughter the role of ethics in business:

"Now imagine that a customer comes into your store and orders a hundred dollars of goods. He pays you with a one-hundred dollar bill and leaves. You suddenly realize that there were *two* one-hundred dollar bills stuck together. Now here is the moral dilemma you have to face: Should you tell your partner or not?"

The Step Ladder Puzzle

You are spending the weekend on a friend's sailboat which is tied to a dock by a long rope. A step ladder attached to the railing of the sailboat has the last two steps under water. With your handy pocket tape measure you determine that each step of the ladder is one-half inch thick and there are nine inches between each step. Now if the tide rises at a constant rate of seven inches per hour, how many steps of the ladder will be under water after three hours?

It's Nothing Like That

Analogies can be used effectively when they draw our attention to perceived similarities between two or more objects or situations. It is reasonable to assume, for the sake of argument, that if two items share some relevant characteristics, then they might also share some other relevant characteristic. Analogies are a type of reasoning that we commonly use in daily life. For example, we use analogical reasoning as the basis for buying or not buying something, based on our own or other people's experience with a product. A great deal of consumer behavior depends on loyalty, so much so that some people continue buying a particular brand of automobile throughout their lives.

Part of the challenge of creating a good analogy is making sure that the things being compared have comparable and relevant characteristics. The phrase "You are comparing apples to asteroids" is a shorthand way of pointing out that a particular analogy is weak (most people don't use the term "asteroids," but perhaps they should). Analogies are often used in science reporting in order to give non-experts a way of grasping abstract ideas. For example, in order to get some rough idea of the structure of atoms, physicists once suggested that we think of the planets orbiting the sun as a way of imagining the relationship of electrons orbiting the nucleus of an atom. Complex scientific principles can be made accessible by a good analogy, as illustrated by the following description:

> The wireless telegraph is not difficult to understand. The ordinary telegraph is like a very long cat. You pull the tail in New York, and it meows in Los Angeles. The wireless is the same, only without the cat.

If you need a more technical explanation of how the wireless telegraph works, then be prepared for some in-depth physics. As for me, I'll stick with the cat.

A good analogy can offer a graphic way of understanding someone's idea. Effective analogies allow us to use our imagination to visually or viscerally experience a different point of view:

> A woman is trying to describe the pain of childbirth to a man who is of the opinion that women tend to exaggerate the amount of pain involved.
>
> The woman says, "Well of course the pain is different for each woman, but let me see if I can help you understand. Take your upper lip and pull it out a little."
>
> "Like this?" asks the man.
>
> "Pull it out some more."
>
> "It's beginning to hurt."
>
> "Okay, now stretch it over your head."

Although analogical reasoning is often effective, it does contain an important weak spot. At best, analogies can offer strong support for an idea, but they cannot completely eliminate the uncertainty involved. For example, a physician might use analogical reasoning when she compares a current patient's set of symptoms to a disease that typically displays similar symptoms. But since one disease can sometimes cause symptoms that overlap with those of another disease, the analogy can never be conclusive. Additional tests can either confirm the diagnosis suggested by the analogy or else rule it out. This example illustrates that analogies rely on shared experiences, memory, and the recognition of relevant patterns. But there are no logically certain guarantees with analogies, simply because two individual objects are never completely identical. Even something as simple as eating several sweet grapes from one bunch can result in the next grape tasting sour.

Speaking of the taste of something, the following story illuminates how imagination can play a big part in how we construct arguments.

> A poor student sat near the curb outside a swanky restaurant as he ate a simple sandwich. He inhaled the great aromas coming from the restaurant and imagined that he was eating in such a fine place.
>
> This routine went on for a week. Finally, the restaurant owner decided to try to put a stop to the student's behavior. The owner approached the student and handed him a bill.

"What's that for?" asked the student.

"You are obviously enjoying the smells coming from my restaurant, so you should pay for them," said the owner.

The student took some coins from his pocket and started shaking and clinking them together in his hands.

"What are you trying to prove?" asked the owner.

"I'm paying you for the smell of the food with the sound of my money," said the student.

Relevance

Analogical reasoning proceeds by adhering to a relatively simple logical structure. It starts by highlighting the common features of two or more things, and then derives a conclusion that the items *probably* have some other feature in common. The driving force of an analogy rests on its ability to get us to agree that the items being compared are similar enough for us to accept the conclusion. The psychological thrust of a good analogy is enhanced by a vivid and graphic picture that is created in our mind. A clever analogy makes us pause for a moment, and challenges us to see where the weaknesses are, as the next example illustrates.

Animals that roam in herds are susceptible to predators. Biology teaches us that the weakest members are the ones most likely to be preyed upon. From the vantage point of natural selection this means that the strongest members will pass on their genes, thus ensuring the overall fitness of the herd.

The human brain is like an animal herd. We know that hard drugs and alcohol kill brain cells. However, like the herd, only the weakest cells are killed off. Therefore, regular use of hard drugs and alcohol successfully removes the weakest brain cells, allowing the best cells to operate more efficiently.

Are you convinced by the analogy? It certainty paints a vivid picture. An important criterion for a good analogical argument is the *relevance* of the characteristics mentioned in the analogy. Some of the characteristics mentioned may have no real bearing on the instance at hand. Look closely at the above example and try to determine whether or not the characteristics mentioned carry any weight when it comes to deciding the strength of the argument.

Just because two things have something in common does not logically require us to accept that what is true of one will be true of the other. Therefore, a strong analogical argument is one where the premises make the conclusion *highly likely* to be true. Every feature in question must be independently checked. Also, irrelevant similarities carry no logical weight. For example, just because two people both have red automobiles, it doesn't necessarily follow that they will get the same gas mileage (one might be a large SUV, while the other might be a hybrid car). Therefore, the issue of the *relevance* of a common feature of two objects is the most important factor by which we determine the force of an analogy.

The good thing about knowing how to spot the weaknesses of analogical arguments is that it can put the person advocating the analogy on the defensive. The following story illustrates this point. It is from Raymond Smullyan's book, *5000 B.C. and Other Philosophical Fantasies*.

> A philosopher went into a closet for ten years to contemplate the question, "What is life?" When he came out, he went into the street and met an old colleague, who asked him where in heaven's name he had been all those years.
>
> "In a closet," he replied. "I wanted to know what life really *is*."
> "And have you found an answer?"
>
> "Yes," he replied. "I think it can best be expressed by saying that life is like a bridge."
> "That's all well and good," replied the colleague, "but can you be a little more explicit? Can you tell me *how* life is like a bridge?"
>
> "Oh," replied the philosopher after some thought, "maybe you're right; perhaps life is not like a bridge."

There goes ten years down the drain. Oh well, back to the closet.

Counteranalogy

It is always logically possible to create a separate analogy in order to counter an already existing analogical argument. The result will be a conclusion that contradicts that of the original argument. Of course, once we have countered the original argument we must then compare the relative strengths and weaknesses of the two competing arguments. However, some counteranalogies are so well done that they expose the original argument and leave it naked to shrivel up like a raisin in the sun:

> At a philosophy conference, a speaker read a paper in which he argued that even though every proof for the existence of God has been shown to be defective, nevertheless the sheer number of proofs should be enough to move us to believe in the existence of God.
>
> A member of the audience responded by saying, "So, if one dead horse can't pull a wagon, then maybe 20 dead horses can."

If the wagon could talk, it might tell us that it appreciates the effort of the 20 dead horses, but it still won't move an inch. The same goes for 20 defective proofs for the existence of God.

Unintended Consequences

Analogies can also be used to show that unintended consequences of an assertion exist. If you can show that an unanticipated and overlooked result follows directly from the person's position, but is completely unacceptable to the person making the assertion, then you can put that person in dire straits. In other words, they wind up painting themselves into a corner. This is nicely illustrated by the following story:

> A convicted felon is asked to make a final statement before sentencing. He says, "I believe that humans don't have free-will. The future is completely determined. Therefore I *did not choose* to commit the

crime, I couldn't help myself. So your honor, you can't send me to prison."

The judge nodded and said, "I am in complete agreement with you that humans don't have free-will. So I would expect you, of all people, to understand that *I'm not choosing* to send you to prison—I can't help myself."

The felon's argument boomeranged back on him. If the felon's claim was correct, then so was the judge's claim. Sometimes a clever argument can turn around and bite us, especially if the person we are dealing with is equally clever.

Groupies

At one time all the sciences were part of the domain of philosophy. Sadly, philosophers have seen their beloved field shrink drastically. Many people, such as Isaac Newton, who did what today we call *physics*, referred to themselves as *natural philosophers*, meaning that they studied nature. Over the years, philosophers have watched stoically as biologists, chemists, astronomers, and all the other natural scientists left to set up their own departments. Then the social sciences began leaving. In addition, recent advances in research have created inter-disciplinary studies dealing with artificial intelligence, cognitive studies, and even consciousness studies. A philosopher once said, "When the next field leaves philosophy, I'm going with it."

Philosophy still has much to contribute to knowledge, and philosophers make great use of the advances in science. In fact, some scientists enlist the help of philosophers to clarify the results of new discoveries. The following story depicts the great working relationship between different academic fields.

An engineer and a philosopher happened to meet while waiting for their flight. They began with the usual small-talk and seemed to hit it off. The engineer said, "It's not often I get to talk to a philosopher.

I've always wanted to know the meaning of life. Can you enlighten me?"

The philosopher answered quickly, "Life is like the complex superstructure of an enormous building."

The engineer was instantly intrigued. He asked, "How is life like the complex superstructure of an enormous building?"

The philosopher said, "I don't know—you're the engineer."

Analogies often compare groups of objects. Of course, there are many ways to refer to the characteristics of a group of objects. Many professions, such as the insurance field, gather massive amounts of information in order to put people into certain groups. For example, how much you pay for life insurance or car insurance depends on the characteristics that place you in a high or low risk group.

Whether or not an object is a member of a group is generally determined by empirical research. Extensive research into anatomy, physiology, and DNA is used to classify many organisms. Similarly, classification methods are used to group together categories of diseases, types of hurricanes, laws, crimes, economic situations, psychological illnesses, and thousands of other designations. Most of these classifications are "naturally occurring" in nature. However, humans have the ability to self-select those groups to which they want to be associated.

There are 10 types of people in the world, those who understand binary and those who don't.

When most people begin reading the joke and see the numeral "10" they immediately think of the number that comes after *nine*. But even in mathematics, certain expressions can have more than one meaning. In the binary system, "10" is used to represent the number *two*. The joke can work only in written form because in binary the expression "10" would have to be pronounced as "one, zero" if spoken aloud.

Here is one more example of the way we classify items:

Every secret can be put into two groups. The first group contains all the secrets that are not worth keeping to yourself. The second group contains all the secrets that are too good to keep to yourself.

We end with a discussion of the *difference* between two groups of objects. Humans are good at finding patterns, and good at discerning fine distinctions between groups. Most humans, anyway:

> A philosophy teacher asked her class to write an essay on the difference between humans and other animals. She was hoping the students would at least be able to write something about obvious accomplishments, such as art, mathematics, complex language, science, and law. Unfortunately, the students were on a different plane of existence. Here are some of their astute responses:
>
> - *Humans have credit cards; animals don't.*
> - *Animals are born with weapons on their bodies, sharp claws and stuff; humans have to make their weapons, bombs and guns and stuff.*
> - *Most humans have sex indoors, but animals do it anywhere.*

Since there are stores devoted exclusively to pets, it's probably just a matter of time until our pets can start carrying their own credit cards (cats will especially like this option). That will nullify the first distinction mentioned above. I'll let you judge the others.

The Mislabeled Boxes Puzzle

Imagine there are three boxes each containing 50 marbles, but there are only two kinds of marbles: red or green. One of the boxes contains *all red marbles*, one box contains *all green marbles*, and one box has *some red and some green marbles*. However, each of the following labels is *incorrect*.

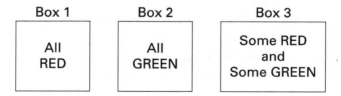

Since each label is incorrect, Box 1 cannot contain all red marbles (it must contain either all green, or some red and some green). Box 2

cannot contain all green marbles (it must contain either all red, or some red and some green). Box 3 cannot contain some red and some green marbles (it must contain either all red or all green).

In order to win a great prize, you are required to determine what each box contains. You are told that you can reach in and pick as many of the marbles from each box that you desire (but you can't look directly into the boxes). At this point, you might think that all you have to do is reach each in and remove one marble at a time until you have removed all the marbles from all three boxes. However, you are also told that there is a way to determine what each box contains *without picking all the marbles*. In fact, you are told there is a *specific number* of marbles that can be picked in order to solve the problem. Can you figure out the *minimum number of marbles* that need to be removed in order to determine exactly what each box contains?

Operator Assistance

There are statements in everyday language that combine two pieces of information, such as, "Soft drinks cause flatulence, and tea contains antioxidants." This *compound* statement contains two *simple* statements: "Soft drinks cause flatulence," and "Tea contains antioxidants." Each of these statements has a truth value (either true or false) independent of the other. When we put the two simple statements together with the word "and" connecting them, we create a *truth-functional statement*. The compound statement has a truth value, too. It is the result of a strictly defined function of the possible truth values of the two simple statements, plus the word "and" which is called a *logical operator* (or logical connective).

Logical operators do not have truth values (they are neither true nor false). This should not be surprising since the word "and" is not a statement. Instead, logical operators work in a way that is similar to mathematical operators. For instance, the mathematical operator "+" has no numerical value; its function is to have us *add* the values to the left and right of it. Likewise, logical operators are understood as alerting us to the type of logical commitments of compound statements. The truth value of a truth-functional statement is determined by the possible truth values of the individual simple statements, together with an understanding of how the logical operator works.

Conjunction

The statement "Soft drinks cause flatulence, and tea contains antioxidants," provides an example of the logical operator called *conjunction*. It consists of the two distinct simple statements, called *conjuncts*, plus the logical operator "and." This logical operator is *strong* in the sense that it requires both conjuncts to be true in order for the compound statement to be true. In other words, if I assert a compound statement using conjunction, then I am claiming that *both* of my simple statements are true. If even one of the simple statements (conjuncts) is false, then the compound statement is false. The only way our example above would be true is if both "Soft drinks cause flatulence" *and* "Tea contains antioxidants" are true at the same time. There is a simple rule for conjunction: *In order for a statement using "and" as the logical operator to be true, it is necessary that both conjuncts be true.*

Of course, there are cases where "and" is used to impart non-truth-functional information:

> I had a lovely room and bath in a hotel on the Las Vegas strip. However, it was a bit inconvenient, because they were in two separate buildings.

The joke is effective because it plays on our expectation and assumption that the room *and* bath are directly connected. The humor results from the realization that our normal expectation has been upended. Here is another example:

> Overheard at a job interview:
> "This year you will get paid $40,000, and next year you will get paid $60,000. So, when would you like to start?"
> "Next year."

The story relies on our everyday knowledge that the word "and" is being used as shorthand. In other words, we interpret the statement as, "This year you will get paid $40,000, *and* if you continue working for us, then next year you will get paid $60,000." Since we expect that the $60,000 salary will be the result of having successfully performed at the job for one year, we are surprised and amused that the interviewee has diverged from our normal expectation.

In logical analysis the order of the individual simple statements makes no difference for a conjunction. The statement, "Soft drinks cause flatulence, and tea contains antioxidants," and the statement, "Tea contains antioxidants, and soft drinks cause flatulence" are logically equivalent. In other words, "A and B" is logically equivalent to "B and A." But this doesn't always work in some daily settings:

> In most cookbooks you will find these kinds of directions: Mix all the ingredients, and bake at 450 degrees for 30 minutes. It will make plenty of difference if you reverse the order: Bake at 450 degrees for 30 minutes, and mix all the ingredients.

Negation

The logical operator "not" refers to the process of *negation*, and it can be understood by considering the following example. Suppose the statement "Dinosaurs became extinct because of constipation" were true. (Don't laugh. There is a hypothesis that suggests the possibility that flowering plants began taking over the dominant position of ferns. Since the dinosaurs depended on ferns for "regularity," the lack of the right dietary ingredient might have brought about their demise.) Okay, let's try to resume our train of thought. If the statement, "Dinosaurs became extinct because of constipation," were true, then its negation, "*It is not the case that* dinosaurs became extinct because of constipation," would be false. The concept of negation is pretty straightforward, but we can sometimes make things more complicated than they need to be:

> At a philosophy lecture, the presenter remarked that there are many instances of two negatives making a positive. For example, in mathematics, multiplying two negative numbers results in a positive number. Also, in English classes we are taught not to use two negatives, such as "I don't got no book."
>
> The presenter then went on to say, "But interestingly enough, there are no instances of two positives making a negative."
>
> Sitting in the audience, the philosopher Sidney Morgenbesser replied sarcastically, "Yeah, yeah."

Morgenbesser had to use only two words to defeat an entire presentation. Now that's an efficient use of language.

Disjunction

A different kind of truth-functional statement uses the word "or" as the logical operator, and it is called *disjunction*. Here is an example: "The Internet is better than fresh-baked bread, or the next U.S. President will be a vegetarian." The two simple statements are called *disjuncts*. We encounter two types of disjunctions in everyday life: inclusive and exclusive. An *inclusive disjunction* is one where it is possible for both disjuncts to be true (or false) at the same time. For example, "Goat milk is a good source of protein, or Puerto Rico will become the 51st state." When we use inclusive disjunction, we are not committed to both statements being true (of course, it is quite all right if both disjuncts are, but it is not necessary). What this means is there is exactly one way for an inclusive disjunction to be false: *both disjuncts must be false at the same time.*

On the other hand, an *exclusive disjunction* is where the truth of one disjunct would *exclude* the other one from being true. For example, "Abraham Lincoln was the 16th President of the United States, or he was the 40th President." If one of the disjuncts is true, then the other cannot be true. In most everyday occurrences, the context reveals which kind of disjunction we are dealing with, if it is not obvious from the statement alone.

Here is an example of a disjunction that you might encounter the next time you travel:

> On a flight from Los Angeles to New York, the flight attendant asks a passenger, "Would you like dinner?"
> The passenger says, "What are my choices?"
> The flight attendant replies, "*Yes* or *No.*"

Conditionals

The truth-functional statement, "If I drank a cup of jasmine green tea after every meal, then I have benefitted from the large amount of antioxidants in each cup," is an example of a *conditional statement*. The statement following the word "if" is referred to as the *antecedent*, and the statement following the word "then" is referred to as the *consequent*. An important factor in recognizing a conditional statement is that the word "if" might not occur at the beginning of a sentence.

> Please notify a flight attendant immediately if you are seated in this row but you cannot read this sign.

That is also a good example of a perfectly self-defeating sign. Here is another one:

> If this sign is under water, then the road is impassable.

In certain situations, a conditional statement might fool us into thinking that an argument has been presented. However, a conditional statement merely asserts that *if* the antecedent is true, *then* so is the consequent. A conditional statement by itself (like other single truth-functional statements) is not an argument.

The logical underpinnings of conditional statements can be quite confusing when we consider their possible truth values. First off, it is crucial to recognize that the word "*if*" is connected only to the antecedent. The assertion goes in one direction, from the antecedent to the consequent. Given this, the only way for a conditional statement to be false is when the antecedent is true but the consequent is false. *Every other combination of truth values makes the conditional statement true.* Using conditionals wisely can sometimes help in awkward situations:

> A girl is going on her first date, so she asks her mother for some things to say in case the conversation stops. The mother, who happens to teach logic, tells her daughter to remember three topics: *food, family,* and *conditional statements.*
>
> While they are eating dinner, the young couple gets stuck in an awkward quiet period. The girl thinks of her mother's advice, and asks the boy, "Do you like anchovies?"
>
> "No, I hate them," said the boy.
>
> "Do you have any brothers?" asks the girl.

"Nope," replies the boy.

Down to her last topic the girl asks, "If you had a brother, would he like anchovies?"

Isn't it nice to know that you can rely on your knowledge of logic to help you out of some awkward situations?

Now comes the tricky part. There is usually some initial difficulty when people realize the full consequences of the above discussion about conditionals. Questions naturally arise when someone begins to analyze what was said earlier: "Given this, the only way for a conditional statement to be false is when the antecedent is true but the consequent is false. *Every other combination of truth values makes the conditional statement true.*" For instance, you might ask, "Why should it be the case that when the antecedent is false, then the conditional statement is true, no matter what the truth value of the consequent?" (Yeah, you would have to ask that question, just when things were going smoothly!) Okay, here is one attempt to make sense of it. Suppose your friends ask you for driving directions from Las Vegas to Los Angeles. You say the following: "If you take I-15 South, then you will come to Los Angeles." Now, if they drive down I-15 South, and it takes them to Los Angeles, then your statement is true. But if they drive down I-15 South, and it does not take them to Los Angeles, then your statement is false. So far, so good.

But what happens if your friends decide to disregard your advice? Suppose they *did not* take I-15 South; they instead took some other road (in that case, the antecedent is false). Two things could happen: Either they get to Los Angeles or they don't (profound, isn't it?). The crucial question for us is what we should now say about your conditional statement. In either case, should your statement be considered false? That seems unfair. After all, you *did not* say that the *only* way to get to Los Angeles is to take I-15 South—you just offered one way to get there. Neither getting to Los Angeles by some other route, nor *not* getting to Los Angeles by some other route should make your conditional statement false, even though in both those instances the antecedent is false (they *did not* take I-15 South). And this takes us back to what was asserted earlier: Since a conditional statement makes a definite assertion about the antecedent, the only way for a conditional statement to be false is if the antecedent is true and the consequent is false. This means that any other combination of truth values will result in the conditional statement being true.

Contingent Statements

Most of the examples we have looked at so far are *contingent statements,* statements that are possibly true or possibly false. A contingent statement such as, "Scientists claim that next winter will be the coldest on record" is neither logically true nor logically false. Instead, its truth value is established through experience of the world.

We are often unaware of how we came to learn things about the world. For example, most young children think of the world as flat. When they are finally told that we live on a spinning spherical object, no child slaps her forehead and exclaims, "Of course, how did I miss that fact!" Most people cannot piece together the slow process that resulted in their finally coming to accept that we do live on a roundish planet, spinning on its axis at around 1,000 miles an hour, and revolving around the Sun at about 65,000 miles an hour. It is not surprising, then, that we tend to miss the amazing learning process that goes on in our children everyday.

Scientific knowledge is tentative. Of course, there are instances where we feel a strong psychological disposition to consider some basic statements as being beyond doubt, such as "I have never been to Mars." Nevertheless, by their very nature, contingent statements are understood as being neither logically necessary nor logically impossible. Here is a story that underscores the logic of contingent statements and their connection to sensory experience:

> A philosopher once imagined that he had his hands in his pockets and someone said the following: "I'll bet that you don't have five fingers on each hand. If I'm wrong, I'll give you $10,000. But if I'm right, you agree to kill yourself." The philosopher admitted that he would be too afraid to take the bet.

The philosopher's position is that past experience is not enough to clinch with certainty that he would win the bet, no matter how psychologically strong the belief was that he had five fingers on each hand. He relied on an argument by the philosopher David Hume. Hume said that the principle of induction can be understood by the following belief: "instances of which we have had no experience resemble those of which we have had experience." In other words, we expect the future to resemble the past because our experience has shown that to be the case. But Hume argued that the principle of induction cannot be proven deductively nor inductively. For example, if we try to argue that the principle of induction is true because it has been reliable in the past, then we commit the circular reasoning fallacy.

Okay, after this discussion, let's return to the philosopher's decision not to take the bet because he was convinced by Hume's analysis of the problem of induction. But how about you? Would you take the bet? If you haven't yet made up your mind, here is a somewhat similar situation, but with a twist:

> Jake told his friends about the night he was walking down a dark alley when all of a sudden a dangerous looking stranger jumped out of the shadows and said, "I'll bet you a hundred bucks that you are dead."
>
> "I was afraid to bet him," said Jake.

The response in the joke is similar to the philosopher's, except that most non-logicians find it funnier. So once again, we can see that humor can reveal some interesting parts of logical reasoning and assumptions.

Non-Contingent Statements

There is something special about the next sentence:

> Potato chips are addictive or potato chips are not addictive.

You probably recognized it as a simple instance of a disjunction, but look more closely. If the first disjunct, "Potato chips are addictive," is true, then the second disjunct, "Potato chips are not addictive," is false (because it is the negation of the first disjunct). This possibility would mean that the disjunction is true. On the other hand, if the first disjunct is false, then the second disjunct is true. This possibility would also mean that the disjunction is true. There are no other possibilities. Thus, it is *logically impossible* for this statement to be false.

This special kind of statement is called a *tautology,* and it reveals a fascinating aspect of logic and language. Whereas contingent statements can be either true or false, tautologies are *necessarily true* by virtue of their logical form (e.g., "P or not P"). No fact about the world could ever make a tautology false. And that's pretty special.

But there is a price to pay. Although they are logically interesting, tautologies are not very helpful for imparting information. For example, suppose you ask your friend whether he will meet you for dinner tonight and he responds, "Either I will be there or I will not be there." Duh! His answer is indeed true; in fact, we now know that it is logically impossible for it to be false. However, has he given you any information? Did you learn anything from his response that you did not already know? Although tautologies are necessarily true, they are not helpful conveyors of information—they are *empty truths.* This is why scientific hypotheses should *not* be tautologies, because then they would be devoid of any possible information about the world—we would never learn anything from them. A hypothesis that is a tautology is trivially true.

Here is another logically interesting sentence:

Diamonds are the hardest substance and diamonds are not the hardest substance.

This is an example of a conjunction, but with a twist. If the first conjunct, "Diamonds are the hardest substance," is true, then the second conjunct, "Diamonds are not the hardest substance," is false (because it is the negation of the first conjunct). This possibility would mean that the conjunction is false. On the other hand, if the first conjunct is false, then the second conjunct is true. This would also result in the conjunction being false. Since there are no other possibilities, it is *logically impossible* for the statement to be true.

This kind of statement is a *self-contradiction,* and it is the flip-side of a tautology. Whereas a tautology is necessarily true, a self-contradiction is necessarily false. Therefore, if we contradict ourselves, then we say something that cannot possibly be true.

Paradox

A paradox often appears at first blush to be a self-contradiction. But you know the old saying, "Things are not always as they appear." The classic example of a paradoxical statement is:

> This sentence is false.

Let's take a closer look at it. On the one hand, if the sentence is true, then what it says is correct. But in that case it is false. (It's okay, you can think about that for a while, if you feel the need. Finished? Then take another deep breath because here comes another wave.) On the other hand, if the sentence is false, then what it says is not correct. But in that case it is true. The paradox seems to logically lead in two directions, each of which cannot be reconciled with the other.

Unlike a self-contradiction, this paradoxical sentence seems to send us on an infinite loop. (If it's true, then it's false. But if it's false, then it's true. But if it's true...) Logicians have tried solving this and other kinds of paradoxical situations for a long time. Although many interesting proposals have been created, none of them has satisfied everyone. This kind of paradox has led some people to argue that there are statements that are *neither* true nor false, while others argue that some statements are *both* true and false.

If you stay alert, then you will be surprised how many times you will come across seemingly paradoxical situations. Here are some hypothetical situations to consider. The first is typical of advertisements that get written without any obvious thinking being done:

Are you illiterate? If so, just write to us for help.

Here is another of the same species:

Are you having difficulty learning math? Just call us at this toll-free number: 1 - 800 - $(x + a)^{n-i} = 1/8\,\pi - [h^2 + \psi\,(x\text{-}7)]$

Finally, one more classic situation to illustrate the point:

I went into a bookstore and asked the salesperson where the self-help books were. She said that if she told me, it would defeat the purpose.

The salesperson believed she was was being helpful by not being helpful. If the customer eventually found the self-help book stacks, then perhaps the salesperson was right. Tough love, anyone?

The Hats Puzzle

On a rainy day with nothing much to do, Joyce, Sandy, and Judy asked their older brother Johnny to give them a game to play. He thought of something that might be fun. He found some old party hats and put them in a bag. The sisters were told that there were only two hat colors, yellow and green, but they were not told how many hats of each color were in the bag. The three sisters sat on the floor, closed their eyes and promised not to peek. Johnny then put a yellow hat on each of their heads. Before they were allowed to open their eyes, Johnny said this: "If any of you see a yellow hat, raise your hand, but don't say anything. As soon as you can figure out what color hat you have on your head, then stand up and explain how you know." They were then told to open their eyes. All three sisters raised their hands. They were silent for quite a while and each had a puzzled look on her face. Suddenly, Joyce stood up and said that she knew that she had a yellow hat on her head, and then began explaining how she knew it.

What explanation did Joyce give? How did she know she had a yellow hat?

Below Average

The ability to make generalizations allows us to create arguments that rely on statistical reasoning. Generalizations rely on the capacity to recognize patterns in nature, which is a valuable survival mechanism. We are not the only animals to use this talent. Dogs and cats will shy away from a food if they connect it to a recent case of illness. However, pattern-seeking can go astray if we misinterpret or exaggerate the weight of evidence. Patterns are often used as premises to argue that a particular order exists in nature. If you argue that a pattern exists without any exceptions, then you are making a *universal generalization*. On the other hand, if you argue that a pattern exists with some exceptions, then you are making a *statistical generalization*.

Here is an example of a universal generalization:

Statisticians have discovered a remarkable fact: *People who have the most birthdays live the longest.*

Those lucky devils! Who knew that longevity was a simple matter tied directly to the number of birthdays we have? In fact, all the researchers had to do was to listen to this wise advice:

Age is not a particularly interesting subject. Anyone can get old. All you have to do is live long enough.

Statistical generalizations are not hard to find. Consider this one:

Statistics have shown that if you were to lay all the statisticians end to end, 66.6% of them would be under water.

Wouldn't it be nice if the government passed a law mandating that all statistical reports had to be funny? But then again, perhaps the government has better things to do with its time.

Statisticians, mathematicians, scientists, and everyday people not only discover new patterns, they also take it upon themselves to offer explanations for why a pattern exists. Statistical arguments can be formally drawn out and brandished with imposing mathematical symbols, or else they can be discussed casually. One type of statistical argument has a generalization as its conclusion. For example:

> The results of a ten-year study were just released. According to the data, smoking is the major cause of statistics.

It is probably true that without the weaknesses of the human flesh, a lot of scientific researchers and statisticians would be out of work.

Another kind of statistical argument uses a generalization as a premise. A lawyer might use this type of reasoning to encourage his client on the best course of action to take:

> A lawyer offered this advice to his client: "Statistics confirm that 50% of all American marriages end in divorce. The answer is obvious. If you do not file for divorce, then your wife will."

Using this kind of reasoning, we can argue that since 50% of all lawyers lie, if a particular lawyer doesn't lie, then his partner does.

If a generalization is used as a premise, then there must be additional supporting evidence that the item under question lies within the scope of the generalization. An adequate explanation for the existence of a generalization requires scientists to provide two things. First, they must describe their research methodology (how they gathered the data). Second, they must offer a roadmap for future testing and discovery.

> Researchers have completed a ten-year study of adult Americans. The results show some interesting statistical facts:
>
> - The average adult American walks approximately 1,000 miles a year.
> - The average adult American drinks approximately 50 gallons of beer a year.
>
> Based on this data, it is clear that adult Americans average 20 miles to a gallon of beer.

The roadmap is clear, and follow-up research cries out for willing experimenters. It is imperative that we find out if hard liquor gets similar results. Plus, we cannot leave out drugs of various kinds. There is a lot of work to be done. Any volunteers?

Samples and Populations

Statistical arguments can be analyzed in two ways. First, we assume that the premises are true (the data). This will tell us the strength of the logical relationship between the premises and the conclusion. Second, we need to examine the accuracy of the claims being made (their truth). For example, we should ask how the statistics were gathered.

> After an exhaustive study, it was finally concluded that 3 out of 4 Americans make up 75% of the population.

That sure seems like a strong and important statistical argument, doesn't it? And it's a good thing they did an "exhaustive" study. After all, a small sample can lead to big errors.

In order to correctly assess a statistical argument, we need to know as much as we can about the research involved. For example, surveys provide samples that are used to make statistical generalizations about populations. A *population* can be any set of objects; it doesn't have to be a human population. A *sample* is a subset of a population. The adequacy of a survey (or any research endeavor, for that matter) depends on the sample. Sample size is one important factor to consider. Generally speaking, the larger the sample size, the better the data (relative to the population size). There are a lot of easy ways to gather large samples, as the next story demonstrates:

> A fire started in a wastebasket at a meeting for the department heads at a university. The head of the physics department told everyone not to panic—he would be able to calculate the amount of energy that had to be eliminated in order to stop the fire.

The head of the chemistry department announced that she would be able to determine the most effective reagent to apply to the fire.

While all this was going on, the head of the statistics department was running around setting fires to all the other wastebaskets in the room.

"What are you doing?" yelled the Dean.

"I'm helping my two colleagues. In order for them to solve the problem, they will need a large sample size."

Random samples are the best kind, because they have the greatest capacity to correctly represent the population. An extended example can show some of the roadblocks on the way to a good survey. Suppose a student is given the assignment of asking other students their opinion regarding the decision to eliminate the school's intermural athletics program due to budget cuts. At the end of the week, the student has recorded the opinions of 10 fellow students. The teacher tells the student that since the school's population is nearly 2,000, the sample size is too small; therefore, it is subject to a possibly large margin of error. The student researcher then collects more data until the sample size reaches 100 students. The teacher commends the student for all the hours spent on the study, *but* (oh, oh, the dreaded "but") the teacher wants to know if the respondents were all seniors. Alas, they were. This admission weakens the ability of the survey to generalize to the entire school. Since the sample is comprised only of seniors, it leaves out everyone else; therefore it is *not* representative of the entire student body—it is a *biased* sample.

Our intrepid student researcher goes back to work and tries to make sure the missing groups are covered. Securing a good spot in the student union cafeteria, the researcher gathers information from equal amounts of first-year, second-year, third-year, and fourth-year students. When the student proudly presents the results, the teacher says, "There is one small problem. Your sample is not random. You surveyed students to which you had easy access. But to get a random sample, you must make sure that *every* member of the student population has an equal chance of getting surveyed. A random sample strengthens the likelihood that the sample represents the population." (Let's hope the student researcher doesn't get too discouraged by all these requirements.)

Here is an example of a piece of research that sounds impressive at first glance:

> Geneticists rely on statistics for much of their work. A recent study that used a large random sample revealed that the number of offspring in humans is an inherited trait. For example, suppose that your biological parents did not have any children. Well, then, the chances are high that you won't, either.

Statisticians are generally careful to avoid making bold claims. They are forever on the lookout for *statistical significance*, which refers to a result that is unlikely to have happened by chance. Extensive documented data is used as the basis for evaluating claims, as portrayed by the next story:

> During the French revolution, a statistician was told that, after one million deaths by guillotine, a miracle happened. A person survived with a completely severed head. The statistician did some quick calculations, shrugged his shoulders and said, "It's not statistically significant."

Averages

There are three different terms that are typically used to describe "average." The first is called the *mean*, and it is the one most of us learn at an early age. It is calculated by adding all the values in a set of data (e.g., the *ages* of the students in a class), and then dividing by the number of items (the *number* of students in the class). Some members of the group will probably be above the calculated average (mean) and some will be below. That is, unless the person doing the math is a politician.

> A person running for office recently made this remarkable claim: "If I'm elected, I give you my sacred vow that every single worker will get an *above average* income."

If the politician can do that, then it would be a miracle. The second method of calculating average is called the *median*. It is arrived at by simply finding the value that separates the group, so that half the group is above the value and the other half is below the value. This in itself is unremarkable, but its application can produce some startling results:

> Did you ever stop to think about the incredible foolishness of the average person? But what's even more remarkable is the fact that, by definition, half the population is even more foolish than that.

There is one more type of average that you should know. The *mode* gets determined by looking for the value (or sometimes values) that occurs most often in a set of data. While all three methods of determining the "average" can be quite accurate, the picture each of them offers is limited in scope. Statistical averages, by themselves, are not very informative of a crucial aspect that usually exists among the members that make up a given set of data—*diversity*. The statistical tool used to exhibit the degree of diversity is called the *standard deviation*, and it can be depicted by a curve. The shape of the curve depicts the overall distribution of the values in a data set. The area at the top of the curve contains the values associated with the *mean*. There is a simple rule of thumb at work here: *the greater the standard deviation, the greater the diversity of the members*. What this tells us is that knowing the "average" can be misleading, unless you are also given the standard deviation, which tells you the amount of diversity among the members of a set. Here is a fantastically clear example:

> A statistician performed an experiment in his kitchen. He put one hand in a bucket of ice and held the other hand over a flame.
>   "Doesn't that hurt?" asked his son.
> "On average, it feels fine."

A lot of research deals with the measurement of "objective" data. For example, you can easily measure the income of every member of your household and then calculate the mean, median, mode, and the standard deviation. The degree of variation among the members can be referred to as "naturally occurring," meaning that it is something that can be objectively measured. In this example, it doesn't matter which country's currency is used, as long as it can be converted to a standard type. But we also know that not everything we want to investigate is this way. This is brought out most clearly by the lengthy controversies over the measurement of human intelligence. Many questions have been asked about the feasibility of trying to measure something that we cannot directly observe. In fact, some have asked whether intelligence is even quantifiable. For example, they point out the disparity in the results of different kinds of intelligence tests, such as ones that rely on reading comprehension skills versus ones that rely on visual skills.

Measuring the "invisible" parts of the world is a challenging part of what science is all about. Scientific breakthroughs have led to enormous changes in our understanding of how the world works. Mastering basic statistical terminology and an appreciation of data-gathering methods are very valuable tools for life in today's complex world. In our everyday lives we are rarely in a position to question the data of a reported piece of research. However, we can digest and scrutinize the *reasoning* involved when the report tries to extend the results to the world outside the sample. As we have seen, arguments can be analyzed without knowing the truth value of the claims being offered. We are constantly being bombarded with statistical information that can tax even the most prepared person.

A U.S. President is at a morning briefing when the Secretary of State makes the following announcement: "We have just received a wire from an embassy in South America. As you know, there has been a lot of military activity recently and it seems to be escalating. An unconfirmed report stated that several Brazilian soldiers have been killed."

The President was stunned. "Oh, my, that's horrible. What a tragedy. I have one question: How many people are in a "brazilian"?

Perhaps basic mathematical literacy should be a requirement for all public office holders. It couldn't hurt.

It should be clear, even from this short discussion of statistics, that research results are not end points. Instead, they are the fountainhead of new questions: Is the world really the way our data suggests? Are the results replicable? Can they be generalized? Should the results affect public policy? These are important questions, and they should be recalled whenever we encounter statistical claims.

We should not be surprised that witty people have used statistical information to create novel and unexpected ways of seeing the world, as illustrated by this story of how things can change drastically over time.

> Two elderly friends are discussing their health. Melanie says, "Do you realize that I've spent more than $3,000 on medical bills in the last two months alone?"
>
> Caroline shook her head and said, "In the good old days you could have been sick for three years for that kind of money."

That's a clever way of showing that statistics and social issues are intimately related. It also shows that some comedy is skillful at seeing how everyday reasoning can be upended by applying unusual and unexpected assumptions.

The Cards Puzzle

Three index cards are placed side by side. Reading from left to right you see the numerals 1, 2, 3, written on top of the cards. You are told that the underside of each card has either the letter P, or the letter Q, or the letter R written on it. Also, the letters are printed either in black, green, or yellow. Each of the letters and colors is used only once. You will be given clues to help you determine which letter and color corresponds to each card.

| 1 | 2 | 3 |

Here are your clues:

1. The P is to the left of the R.
2. The yellow letter is to the right of the black letter.
3. The green letter is to the left of the Q.
4. The Q is to the left of the R.

Your assignment, should you choose to accept it, is to determine which colored letter is under each card.

Casual Causality

When we start a sentence with the word "Why" we are probably going to ask for an explanation of something. Events, behaviors, and recognized patterns are *effects*, and they get explained when we discover the underlying *causes*. Scientists naturally look for causes, but so do non-scientists. If a lamp in your bedroom doesn't work, then you will look for the cause. You might check to see if the light bulb has burned out, or check to see if the lamp is plugged in correctly. These actions are similar to what a scientist does in a laboratory, but without all the expensive equipment, huge research grants, graduate assistants, potential Nobel Prize, (okay, maybe they are not that similar, but the underlying principles are the same—the search for causes).

Empirical research lies at the heart of the investigation of cause-effect relationships. Well-designed experiments can help either *confirm* (support) or *disconfirm* (refute) the existence of a cause-effect relationship. For example, experiments used in drug testing should follow specific guidelines in order to eliminate possible bias. The subjects, as well as those administering the drugs and the placebos, should be kept in the dark as to which subjects are getting the drug. In everyday life you might try using a new kind of vitamin for a month to see if you feel any different. On another occasion, you might want to know why you have a severe stomachache: "What did I eat or drink today that might have caused it?"

The underlying mechanisms of cause-effect relationships are not difficult to understand. An important ingredient to making sense of the concept of *causality* is the ability to uncover necessary and sufficient conditions. A *sufficient condition* is when one event always brings about another event. The logic involved in a sufficient condition can be grasped by looking at how we use conditional statements in particular contexts. For example, a doctor might say, "If you take this medicine as prescribed, then you will get better." The physician is making a causal claim by asserting that taking the medicine will be sufficient to cure your illness. In other words, according to the doctor, this single prescription is enough to do the job. Of course, the claim offers only a *potential* sufficient condition since you will have to wait until you finish taking the medicine to see if it worked. Here is an example of an unexpected sufficient condition:

> A woman asks her doctor for a prescription for birth control pills. The doctor says, "But you don't need them. You're past the childbearing age."
>
> The woman replies, "Oh, I know that. I just need them to help me sleep."
>
> "But they won't work as sleeping pills," says the doctor.
>
> "Sure they will," answers the woman. "I'm going to start putting them in my daughter's morning orange juice, so I can sleep better at night."

The mother is wisely asserting that giving her daughter birth control pills is a sufficient (and safe) condition for the mother to be able to get a good night's sleep.

Another simple example of a sufficient condition is the claim, "If my television comes on, then electricity is being sent to the television." It would be strange for someone to be watching a TV program and suddenly doubt that electricity was getting to the television. But what about this case: "If electricity is being sent to the television, then my television will come on." If it is true that electricity is getting to the television, then does this guarantee that your television will come on? It doesn't, because there are other things that have to be working. In fact, there are many parts that make up the television set that all have to be in working order for it to come on. Although having your television come on is a *sufficient condition* for there being electricity, having electricity is *not a sufficient condition* for the television coming on. Therefore, in order to determine if a sufficient condition exists you need to ask if one event *guarantees* that another event will occur. If your analysis shows that it does, then a sufficient condition exists.

The logic underlying a *necessary condition* is not difficult to comprehend. We typically use the term "necessary" to emphasize that one thing or event is required, essential, or mandatory for some other thing or event to occur. Here are some simple examples:

1. Oxygen is required for human survival.
2. You must have at least 124 credits to graduate from our college.
3. You cannot drive legally unless you have a valid driver's license.
4. A sense of humor requires a brain.

Uncovering necessary conditions is an important part of learning about cause-effect relationships. Let's use the example from earlier to explore other aspects of necessary conditions: "If my television comes on, then electricity is being sent to the television." We saw that electricity was not sufficient for the television to come on. However, since the television will not work without it, then electricity is a necessary condition. Therefore, in order to determine if a necessary condition exists, you need to ask if the *absence* of one event *guarantees* that another will *not* occur. If your analysis shows that this is the case, then a necessary condition exists.

Discovering a necessary condition, by itself, is not enough to establish that a cause-effect relationship exists. Here is one clear example:

Scientists have uncovered the major cause of divorce—*marriage*.

Although you can't get divorced unless you are married (it is a necessary condition), merely being married is not a sufficient condition for getting a divorce. Looking for the reasons why something occurs is the rationale for all investigations of causality. In order to establish a true cause-effect relationship, scientists look for both necessary and sufficient conditions. In the following story, a doctor, relying on years of experience and a thorough knowledge of medicine, quickly locates the cause of a patient's pain.

A man goes to the doctor complaining that his whole body hurts. As proof, the man pokes his finger against his head and screams in pain.

Then he pushes his finger into his chest and yelps again. Finally, when he prods his finger into his leg, tears run down his cheeks. "What's wrong with me, doc?"

"It's really quite simple. Your finger is broken."

Causal Networks

Now that the preliminaries are over, let's look at a simple case of causality. Suppose that you accidently drop a cup and it shatters when it hits the floor. Applying scientific reasoning, you judge that the simple cause of the shattered cup was its impact with the floor. Now this is certainly a normal reading of the case. However, suppose you wanted a deeper appreciation of the causality involved. You might get some more cups and do some experiments. You begin working with the idea that a similar cup dropped on the floor will get the same result. In other words, you are using a basic scientific principle: *same cause, same effect*.

However, instead of just dropping another cup in the same manner, you decide to change some variables. You bend down and throw a cup at a sharp angle to the floor and, lo and behold, the cup doesn't break. Next, you place a pillow on the floor, drop a cup, and once again it doesn't break. Finally, you get a cup with a similar shape and weight, but made of aluminum, drop it on the floor and it, too, does not break.

These experiments allow us to expand our knowledge of "the cause" of the broken cup to include the idea of a *causal network*, the set of necessary and sufficient conditions that make up the overall cause. When you changed the variables making up the original event you brought about different results. In addition (provided you have enough cups), you eventually will learn to eliminate variables that are not necessary for the effect, such as whether it is day or night, the amount of illumination in the room, the color of the cup, among other things. This procedure illustrates the painstaking nature of causal research. The method is exemplified by the budding scientist in the next story:

Two college buddies are talking about the upcoming spring break.

"So where are you going," asks Brad.

"To Russia," answers Clayton.

"Didn't you go there last year, too."

"Yeah, I did. But this year I'm taking my own radio, so I'll have a better time."

"Why is that," asks Brad.

"Because all the radios there play nothing but Russian music."

Imagine how surprised Clayton will be when he turns on his radio in a Moscow hotel room. But being a true scientist, he will eventually hit upon a solution.

Causes are investigated from the standpoint of the *normal state* of a system, which is just the historical data regarding the item in question. In the cup example, the persistence of an unbroken condition is called the *normal state of the cup*. When the cup shattered, an *abnormal state* was established. The drastic change in the state of the cup required a causal explanation. The subsequent experiments helped establish the causal network by which the abnormal state was created. However, sometimes achieving an abnormal state is mere wishful thinking, as the next story highlights:

A patient asks the optometrist, "Will I be able to read with these new glasses?"

The optometrist says, "Sure you will."

The patient says, "That's great. I never knew how to read before."

There are additional features to causality that need to be introduced. The *precipitating cause* is the direct causal network that brings about an event. In the cup example, it includes all the factors that contributed to the event. Complementing the idea of a precipitating cause, a *remote cause* is a past event that is connected to the event in question. In our cup example, a remote cause of your having dropped the cup might be a scream or other loud noise that startled you. A remote cause is typically not considered a direct part of the scientific explanation of the physical event. However, if we were interested in assigning blame for legal purposes, we would certainly consider any important remote causes. For example, a hired killer is the precipitating cause of a murder, but the person hiring the killer is the remote cause (both would be legally responsible for the murder).

Humans are great at thinking of possible complex causal networks. But no matter how plausible they may sound, they can clearly illustrate the complexity involved in unpacking causal networks. The interweaving of several aspects of causal analysis should instill in us a cautious approach to making causal claims. When we understand that most real-life situations involve interlocking pieces of a vast causal web, then we become more careful in making final decisions, especially when those decisions impact large portions of society. The next story embodies the dual aspects of *precipitating* and *remote* causes.

> A man came into an emergency room and said that he had broken his arm. "How did it happen," asked the admitting nurse.
>
> "About eight years ago, I ..." The nurse interrupted him and said, "No, no, just tell me how you broke it today."
>
> "That's what I'm trying to do," said the man. "About eight years ago, I was offered a chance to buy Bitcoins for 39 cents each. I laughed at the whole idea of cryptocurrencies and declined the offer." Clearly agitated, the nurse said, "I hate to interrupt you again, but what does any of this have to do with your broken arm?"
>
> "I'm coming to that. This morning when I was driving to work I heard on the radio that Bitcoins were selling for $10,000 each. I slapped myself in the forehead, lost control of the car and crashed."

Issues regarding causality appear in numerous settings. For example, if your cat is ill you might take it to the vet. If the precipitating cause is revealed to be poison, then you will probably investigate further. Was it a nasty neighbor, or was it caused by a bad can of cat food? If it was a neighbor, then you might attempt to find out what caused the neighbor to do it. On the other hand, if it was the cat food, then you might notify the manufacturer to see if it is an isolated case, or a more general quality-control issue.

Correlations

Another kind of scientific approach is to look for the common ingredient in cases of related effects. For example, if four people eat at a restaurant and they get sick, then they might list the things they had in common to see if one item stands out. Pinpointing a precipitating cause can sometimes be a matter of simple elimination. Nevertheless, it must be done carefully and with a heavy dose of common-sense:

> A person woke up three mornings in a row with a terrible hangover. He carefully listed what he had the three previous nights: gin and tonic water, vodka and tonic water, and whisky and tonic water. He concluded that the tonic water caused the hangovers.

The three hangover effects were certainly all correlated with the tonic water, but they also were correlated with alcohol, which was erroneously dismissed. This illustrates another important concept in scientific research. A *correlation* is a statistical connection between two or more events, and although it is a *necessary* ingredient for causality, it is *not sufficient* to prove causation. At best a correlation reveals a possible case of causation. Many superstitions were formed because of a simple case of correlation between an otherwise innocuous event and the occurrence of something bad. The chance connection between two events can easily get ingrained in the belief system of a group, with the result that it is passed on to later generations who accept uncritically the traditional belief.

> A superstitious grandfather told his grandson, "A cat crossing your path during a full moon is a sign."
> Upon hearing this, the grandmother said, "Yeah, it means that the cat is going somewhere."

When we discover the mechanisms involved in cause-effect relationships, we gain the ability to predict a small part of the future. Causality is a complex issue that requires knowledge and understanding of interrelated connections. Discovering a cause-effect relationship doesn't end an investigation, it is really just the beginning. It impels us to create theories, hypotheses, and additional experiments that will fill in missing pieces of the puzzle. Scientists know that even the most intriguing results are best considered tentative. The future might resemble the past, but it won't be exactly the same. As my friend Jerzy once said, "The future is like the present, only longer."

> A receptionist went up to a patient in the waiting room of a doctor's office and said, "I'm glad you're here, Mr. Kolodziej. There seems to be a problem with your outstanding bill. According to our records, your check came back."
>
> Mr. Kolodziej replied, "So did my arthritis."

The history of science shows that even our best theories and knowledge can be overthrown by new discoveries. The tentative nature of science is the driving force behind all research. Scientists push knowledge to its limits in order to discover better answers in the same way that researchers test products far beyond their normal use in order to create better products.

Our discussion of causality reveals some important aspects of the role of explanations. A causal explanation provides a way for further exploration by suggesting avenues leading to additional corroborating evidence. In this way, a fruitful explanation can lead to the discovery of new facts about the world.

The terms "explanation" and "hypothesis" are often used interchangeably. A *hypothesis* is a conjecture about a single event or a series of related events. For example, a company might try to explain why one of their electric cars caught on fire, or a government research team might investigate why a series of similar fires occurred in different models of electric cars. Since a hypothesis is a *statement* that provides an explanation of an event, we can say that hypotheses are either true or false. For instance, based on a preliminary investigation of a crime, a detective might offer a tentative hypothesis regarding *who did it*. This gives the detective a focus for gathering additional evidence to establish the truth or falsity of her hypothesis.

The fact that a hypothesis is a *statement* provides a way of distinguishing it from a theory. A *theory* generally consists of a *set of definitions* about a range of phenomena, and it can be thought of as an abstract tool. For example, in physics, Isaac Newton's major theory deals with "particles in motion" and it defines terms such as "momentum" and "mass." In biology, Gregor Mendel's theory of "inheritance" includes definitions of "dominant" and "recessive" traits. In this sense, theories offer a manual for how to use an abstract tool, and like other tools they can prove to be useful, or even quite useless, for solving our problems. Scientist's use theories to construct hypotheses which they can test.

We tend to call the greatest scientists "geniuses" because their ideas changed the way we view the world and our place in it. The brains of some of the most famous scientists have been dissected with the hope of discovering something unique that all geniuses possess and which mere mortals lack. Nothing definitive has been found. But we do know that quite often the genius spark reveals itself early in life. Accepting that fact can be a source of hope or despair, depending on your age.

Returning to the example above, the detective probably relies on several *theories* when confronted with a specific crime. For example, one theory of crime might emphasize emotions, while another might stress possible gain as the motive. The detective has a toolkit of crime theories, and like an expert in any field, a good detective will take the preliminary clues and begin applying a particular theory to help solve the crime. Of course, the detective might apply the wrong theory, resulting in a dead end. (This is similar to a car mechanic who thinks that you have a mechanical problem, only to find out later that the problem was electrical.) Once the detective has settled on a particular theory to apply to the crime, she will be in a position to offer a hypothesis—*Mr. Mustard is the killer*—which is either true or false. So, the next time you hear a detective in a movie say, "I have theory who the killer is" you can rewrite the script because the detective really has a hypothesis that may or may not be correct.

Whereas *theoretical science* searches for grand explanations for what we observe, *experimental science* does the nuts and bolts of laboratory work. Theory and experiment form a symbiotic relationship. A new theory can offer experimenters new ideas to test. On the other hand, inventions and breakthroughs in advanced technology often leads to unexpected new experimental data that challenges theorists to offer explanations or new theories. Our scientific understanding of the world develops through a constant evolution of knowledge.

> A physics teacher accidently overheard a student say to a small group of fellow students that he was able to get his hands on a copy of the upcoming final exam in physics. "Guess what? The questions are exactly the same as last year's exam, so we can't miss," said the student.
>
> The teacher announced to the startled group, "If you had been coming to class all semester, then you would have learned that research in physics advances rapidly, causing us to revise our knowledge of how the world works. So, although all the questions for this year's final exam are indeed the same as last year, I'm sorry to disappoint you, but this year all the answers are different."

Testing Hypotheses

Hypotheses are often easily proposed, but they can sometimes be notoriously difficult to test. The simplest and surest method of testing a hypothesis is through a well-developed, *controlled experiment*, which attempts to isolate one variable. A laboratory setting allows strict control over potentially competing variables, and permits researchers to concentrate on the effect of one variable at a time. Contrast this controlled setting with naturally occurring, complex real-life situations with dozens of variables acting at the same time, thus making it difficult to hit upon a correct cause-effect relationship.

The results of prolonged and repeatable experiments are what allow scientists to make accurate predictions. Nevertheless, the artificial nature of the laboratory setting is part of the reason why scientific results cannot always be projected accurately onto the real-world. In addition, drug experiments on some animals may prove fruitful in the laboratory, but the results may not be transferable to humans. This is why the results of scientific research are tentative.

Before a hypothesis is accepted, it needs to undergo rigorous testing. There are several criteria that must be met in order to establish a causal relationship.

1. A *correlation* exists between the *cause* and the *effect*.
2. The cause *precedes* an effect.
3. The cause is in the *proximity* of the effect.
4. A set of *necessary* and *sufficient* conditions exists.
5. *Alternative explanations* are ruled out.

Although each of the criteria is *necessary* to establish a causal relationship, each one individually is *not sufficient* to establish a cause-effect relationship. It takes the cumulative weight of the evidence for the criteria to establish a solid causal claim. Since we can be distracted by a single dazzling result, we must remain ever vigilant.

Although a correlation is one of the necessary conditions for a cause-effect relationship, it often is used mistakenly in isolation to make a causal claim (recall the "tonic water" example). However, the error is often easily revealed. For example, although there is a very strong correlation between certain barometer readings and storms, we know that the former does not cause the latter. There is also a high correlation between people wearing swimsuits and getting suntans, but the swimsuit does not cause the suntan.

The second criterion above focuses our attention on the length of time between the onset of the cause and the subsequent effect. If there is an inordinate time lapse between the onset of a suspected cause and an effect, then the chances are increased that other variables may have affected the outcome. The idea behind the third criterion is that a large spatial distance between the suspected cause and the effect allows other variables to interfere in the process. The fourth criterion requires us to have a firm understanding of both the sufficient and the necessary conditions for bringing about the effect. Finally, the fifth criterion stresses the necessity of eliminating plausible alternative (rival) explanations. Since a causal assertion can be undermined by alternative potential causes, the alternatives must be ruled out. The ability to successfully accomplish these tasks is embedded in the general strategy of a controlled experiment, one designed to isolate and eliminate the effects of every variable except one.

A hypothesis is created in order to present a possible causal relationship. But many of the most interesting hypotheses are not readily subject to simple, direct, and immediate testing. Even though a hypothesis, by definition, asserts something that is either true or false (e.g., "Sam Marlowe committed the murder"), it often requires considerable ingenuity to get the world to reveal its secrets. Although the strategy and principles behind experimental research is quite rational, some applications of it are ironic.

> Many "holistic and alternative health" experts claim that modern medicine is not trustworthy. Nevertheless, they are quick to point out that their products have gone through extensive laboratory testing.

A hypothesis is often developed to explain a particular body of known facts. Therefore, hypothesis testing requires extending the reach of the initial assertion. In those instances, we need to think of a situation that forces the hypothesis into a new area. A scenario needs to be imagined that will get the person advocating for the hypothesis to make a prediction. This will help us uncover new facts that will either support or undermine the hypothesis. This is accomplished by asking the question, "What if we were to do this experiment?" A simple illustration should suffice. If the kitchen light does not come on when you flip the switch, then someone might hypothesize that the light bulb is burned out. This conjecture can be tested by replacing the bulb with a new one. The person who made the light bulb hypothesis should predict that the light will now work. There are two possible results: First, if the light does come on, then the *prediction is true* and the *hypothesis is confirmed.* Second, if the light does not come on, then the *prediction is false* and the *hypothesis is refuted.*

> A skeptic of supernatural abilities is giving a public lecture and asks the audience, "Will all those who believe in telekinesis, please raise my hand."

The simple kitchen-light example requires further discussion. The words "confirmed" and "refuted" are not to be taken as absolutes. Suppose that the hypothesized "bad" light bulb was in fact *not* defective. It could have been that the bulb had loosened just enough to prevent contact with the electric element in the socket. Therefore, although replacing the "bad" bulb with a new bulb that was properly screwed in *confirmed* the hypothesis, it did not definitively answer the question. Additional confirmation is usually needed to support a hypothesis. For example, we could take the so-called bad light bulb and screw it back into the socket to verify the initial results. This is also the procedure for the case of *refutation* (disconfirming). In our example, the new light bulb could be defective, so once again, the refuting instance should not be considered definitive. In both cases, we might want to try the original bulb in a different location. This is why researchers do multiple experiments under a variety of settings. They generally do not consider one confirmation or refutation as the end of the discussion.

Sometimes people refuse to accept the defeat of their hypothesis, as the next example illustrates.

> Two roommates are having breakfast when one says, "It is a scientific fact that if you drop a buttered piece of bread, then it will always land butter side down."
>
> "I don't believe that. Surely sometimes it must land butter side up."
>
> "No, it never will. I'll prove it to you." He puts butter on a piece of bread, drops it, but it lands butter side up.
>
> "Ha, I was right. It's not a scientific fact."
>
> "No, it is a fact."
>
> "But your experiment just refuted your own hypothesis."
>
> "No, I did the experiment wrong."
>
> "What do you mean?"
>
> "I put the butter on the wrong side of the bread."

The predictive ability of a hypothesis is a crucial determinant of its usefulness. Predictions are the backbone of decision-making regarding our understanding of the world. We often challenge someone's assertion by asking them to back it up ("Do you want to bet?"). In most cases, the result of a single experiment is usually not solid grounds for accepting or rejecting a hypothesis. However, the overall consideration of the value of a hypothesis rests squarely on the shoulders of the predictions associated with that hypothesis.

There are degrees of acceptability of evidence. We often need to make fine distinctions about the *relevance* of evidence, and we must have strong reasons to eliminate any evidence that is deemed to be irrelevant. That means criteria must be available to determine the amount of weight to assign to a given piece of evidence. There are three simple requirements that help to accurately decide the weight of evidence. In order to ensure an honest test of a hypothesis, we need a way to distinguish acceptable from unacceptable predictions.

1. There must be a way to objectively *verify* the results of the experiment.
2. The prediction must *not* be *trivial*.
3. The prediction must be a *logical consequence* of the hypothesis.

Let's look at the requirements one by one. The first requirement spells out the necessity for unambiguous results. Of course, the unambiguous nature of evidence is sometimes dependent on the setting.

Two American students and their professor are at a convention in France when they decide to take a walk in the country. On a hillside, they spot a single grazing black sheep. The undergraduate student announces, "Aha, the sheep in France are black."

The graduate student replies, "No, all we can say for sure is that *at least one* of the sheep in France is black."

The professor patiently explains that, "The truth of the matter is that there is *at least one* sheep in France that is black *on one side*."

A local farmer who had been listening to the conversation said, "In France, we say that there *appears* to be some object that can be described as a sheep that also *appears* to be black on one side."

Who knew that at least one farmer in France was a natural philosopher? Or maybe we should say that it *appears* that some object that can be described as a French farmer also *appears* to be a natural philosopher, based on his one statement. Whew, that's tiring (but it is clear, isn't it?).

Let's consider another hypothetical case: Imagine that several small children were getting sick in a particular apartment building. Two neighbors develop alternative hypotheses:

Jane   The paint used in the apartments has a high lead content.

Steve   There are poltergeists in the apartments.

Depending on your beliefs, you might have smiled at Steve's hypothesis. But both hypotheses start out the same; that is, they both make assertions that are either true or false. The ability to secure reliable results will ultimately separate the two hypotheses. Notice that neither hypothesis mentions something that can be decided at face value, since they both refer to objects that are invisible to the naked eye. What distinguishes the two hypotheses is the capacity for reliable testing. Jane's hypothesis allows us to predict that if we take a paint sample to a laboratory, then we should find high levels of lead. If the results verify the prediction, then the evidence supports her hypothesis. However, if there is no trace of lead in the paint, or if the amount of lead is within safety limits, then the prediction is false and the evidence refutes her hypothesis. This underscores the first requirement that a prediction must be *verifiable* (a method exists to objectively decide whether the prediction is true or false).

Now let's turn to Steve's hypothesis. There is no certifiably objective method to determine the presence of poltergeists (outside of the movie *Ghostbusters*). Of course, Steve might complain that we are being unfair, since poltergeists are invisible to the naked eye. But so is the lead in the paint; yet we could easily get verifiable evidence regarding Jane's hypothesis. Also, whereas we have additional scientific information to explain why excessive lead in paint can cause sickness, there are no comparable reasonable explanations for how a non-physical object (a poltergeist) could affect a physical object.

> A man is staggering down the street carrying a cardboard box. A police officer stops him and says, "You are obviously drunk. What have you got in the box?"

"It's a mongoose. When I get real drunk I start seeing snakes and I get scared, so I have the mongoose for protection."

The police officer smiles and says, "Don't you realize that the snakes are only imaginary?"

"I know, but so is the mongoose."

We can now consider the second requirement (the prediction must not be trivial). A prediction that is not trivial gets evaluated by reference to what we already know. This body of facts is referred to as "background knowledge." Whether or not a prediction is considered trivial rests on what we expect to happen. For example, imagine that I claim to be able to see future events. This assertion is either true or false. But recalling our discussion of the first requirement above, you quickly request that I provide some objective and verifiable evidence. I agree to the challenge. I predict that someone will be born today. This is certainly a verifiable prediction, and, since it will surely be true, it illustrates why the first requirement, by itself, is not strong enough to eliminate my trivial prediction. The second requirement successfully eliminates such trivial predictions and declares that they are irrelevant. Since this requirement forces me to revise my strategy to prove to you that I can foresee the future, I hereby offer a new prediction as evidence:

There will be 74 children born in Pittsburgh, Pennsylvania tomorrow. Of these, 39 will be girls and 35 boys. Oh, by the way, among the 74, there will be six sets of twins.

Is the prediction verifiable? *Yes*. Is it trivial? *No*. You would not expect such a specific prediction to turn out to be true. And for the very reason that we expect it to be false, it will prove to be a good test of my hypothesis. And this is exactly what the second requirement asks. This ensures that when my prediction turns out to be false, you will have strong objective evidence that refutes the hypothesis that I can foresee the future.

We can easily find examples of hypothesis testing that are used to gather important information, as the following story illustrates.

A group of pre-med students are on a field-trip to a psychiatric hospital. A student asks one of the staff how they decide whether a patient is ready to be released.

"They have to pass a test. We present them with a bathtub full of water. Then we show them a spoon, a cup, and a bucket, and ask them the quickest way to empty the bathtub."

The student says, "I understand. A patient is normal if he or she knows that the correct answer is the bucket."

The staff member replies, "No, a patient is normal if he or she says, *Take out the drain plug.*"

The third requirement (the prediction must be a logical consequence of the hypothesis) ensures that a direct connection exists between the hypothesis and the prediction. We want to be able to take the final truth value of the prediction and attach it to the hypothesis.

In one of the old *Ma and Pa Kettle* movies, Ma says, "How many times have I told you to get those pigs out of the house. It's not healthy."

Pa says, "Aw, go on. Those pigs have never been sick a day in their lives."

Predictions don't come out of thin air. They are the offspring of a fertile hypothesis and a viable experiment. The fledgling predictions may or may not survive the cruel world. They exist as possible confirmations or refutations of the hypothesis. We should regard the process as confronting nature with questions and watching for clear answers. Knowledge requires patience and an accumulation of evidence. If we make mistakes, they will be revealed by the results of repeated experiments.

Light from an object travels to our eyes at an incredible 186,000 miles per second. By way of comparison, sound travels to our ears at a slow 1,125 feet per second. Maybe that explains why some people first *appear* to be bright—that is, until we hear them speak.

This takes us back to where we started: *Logical reasoning and humor have an interesting relationship.*

The Gallons Puzzle

You have signed up for a psychology experiment that will test various cognitive abilities. The first test seems relatively simple. You are given a three-gallon bucket and a five-gallon bucket. You can fill the buckets with water from a sink. You job is to get exactly four gallons of water in the five-gallon bucket. Can you figure out how to do it?

Puzzle Solutions

Chapter 1 The Cake Puzzle

For most people, the puzzle creates in their minds a decidedly two-dimensional view of the world and the cake. The two illustrations have us looking down on the cake. Given this perspective, we could easily fail to see a way out of the problem because we are stuck thinking that the cuts must always be made vertically. But there was a hint offered by the sentence, "Now the plot thickens." In other words, you need to imagine the cake as a three-dimensional object. Once you realize this, you can see that a horizontal cut of the cake through its middle will leave four pieces on top and four on the bottom, all equal to each other.

Chapter 2 The Start-Finish Puzzle

Since both races started at exactly 9:00 a.m., you must have passed one spot at the exact same time on both days. To see this, simply draw a line to illustrate a path from the start line to the finish line. Next, put one finger on the start line and another finger on the finish line, then start moving them toward each other. To simulate the relative speeds of each race, you can move the finger from the start side faster than the finger from the finish side. But no matter how fast or slow you move your fingers, they will always cross each other at some point.

Chapter 3 The Portrait Puzzle

Most people immediately guess that it is Carly herself who is in the portrait; but that is incorrect. Carly's statement refers to "the mother of the young girl in the portrait" as being "my mother's daughter." Now the phrase, "my mother's daughter" can refer only to Carly, because she says "I have no sisters or brothers." Given this, "the *mother* of the young girl in the portrait" must be Carly. Therefore, the young girl in the portrait is Carly's daughter.

Chapter 4 The Step Ladder Puzzle

The same two steps will be under water. As the tide rises, the sailboat will rise with it, along with the step ladder which is attached to the sailboat.

Chapter 5 The Mislabeled Boxes Puzzle

The problem can be solved simply by picking *one marble*, but it must be from Box 3 ("Some RED and Some GREEN"). Since each marble can be either red or green, let's suppose that you reach into Box 3 and pick a red marble. Since Box 3 is mislabeled, it must contain all red marbles. Given this, Box 2 ("All GREEN") must contain some red and some green marbles. This follows because if Box 1 contained some red and some green, then Box 2 would contain all green marbles, but this can't be right because each label is incorrect.

The other possibility is that you that you reach into Box 3 and pick a green marble. Since Box 3 is mislabeled ("Some RED and Some GREEN"), it must contain all green marbles. Given this, Box 1 ("All RED") must contain some red and some green marbles. This follows because if Box 2 contained some red and some green, then Box 1 would contain all red marbles, but this can't be right because each label is incorrect.

Chapter 6 The Hats Puzzle

Joyce reasons as follows: All three of us have raised our hands, so we must all see at least one yellow hat. I see a yellow hat on both Sandy and

Judy, but what do they see? Sandy sees Judy's yellow hat and Judy sees Sandy's yellow hat. But what do they see on me? Suppose I am wearing a green hat. If so, then Sandy would see my green hat and she would quickly realize that she had to have a yellow hat, because Judy raised her hand. The same result holds from Judy's point of view. So, if I were wearing a green hat, both Sandy and Judy should have stood up by now. Since neither one has stood up, I conclude that I *cannot* be wearing a green hat; I must be wearing a yellow hat.

Chapter 7 The Cards Puzzle

We can combine the information in Clue 3 with the information in Clue 4. If the green letter is to the left of the Q, and the Q is to the left of the R, then we can conclude that the correct order must be the following: The green letter is under Card 1, the Q is under Card 2, and the R is under Card 3. We also know that the P must be under Card 1, and it is green.

Since Clue 2 asserts that the yellow letter is to the right of the black letter, we can conclude that a black Q is under Card 2, and a yellow R is under Card 3. Therefore, the final answer is: Card 1: Green P; Card 2: Black Q; Card 3: Yellow R.

Chapter 8 The Gallons Puzzle

First, fill the five-gallon bucket to the top. Use the water in the five-gallon bucket to fill the three-gallon bucket to the top. Two gallons will then remain in the five-gallon bucket. Take the three-gallon bucket of water and empty it into the sink. Then pour the two gallons that are in the five-gallon bucket into the three-gallon bucket. Now fill the five-gallon bucket to the top once again. Then pour one gallon from the five-gallon bucket into the three-gallon bucket (this will fill it to the top). You now have exactly four gallons left in the five-gallon bucket.

About The Title

The remaining task is to try to answer the question that is the title of the book: *Why Did the Logician Cross the Road?* I'm sure that by now you have thought of several clever answers. But perhaps we can simply adopt the wisdom imparted by Professor Irwin Corey in Chapter 4: *Well, that's a two-part question. The first part, "Why?"* ...

Suggestions For Further Reading

The following is offered for readers who might want to explore the topics introduced in this book. The list can get you started. Most of the items will refer you to other books or articles. Some of the material concentrates on specific topics, such as theories of humor, fallacious reasoning, the psychology of jokes, and logic puzzles. Since many of the books have gone through several editions and publishers, we provide one reference to get you started.

Introduction to Logic Textbook

Stan Baronett, *Logic* 5e, Oxford University Press, 2021, provides comprehensive explanations of all the topics introduced in this book, including informal logic, deductive logic, and inductive logic.

Informal Logic and Critical Thinking

Mark Battersby, *Is That a Fact? A Field Guide for Evaluating Statistical and Scientific Information*, Broadview Press, 2009.

M. Neil Browne and Stuart M. Keeley, *Asking the Right Questions: A Guide to Critical Thinking,* Pearson College, 2000.

Leo Groarke and Christopher Tindale, *Good Reasoning Matters!*, Oxford University Press, 2012.

David Morrow, *Giving Reasons*, Hackett Publishing, 2017.

Lewis Vaughn, *Critical Thinking* 6e, Oxford University Press, 2018.

Inductive Logic

Ian Hacking, *An Introduction to Probability and Inductive Logic*, Cambridge University Press, 2001.

Deborah G. Mayo, *Error and the Growth of Experimental Knowledge*, University of Chicago Press, 1996.

Nicholas Rescher, *Luck: The Brilliant Randomness of Everyday Life,* University of Pittsburgh Press, 2001.

Paul Rosenbaum, *Observation and Experiment: An Introduction to Causal Inference*, Harvard University Press, 2019.

Theories of Humor

Henri Bergson, *Laughter: An Essay on the Meaning of the Comic*, The Macmillan Company, 1911.
Sigmund Freud, *Jokes and Their Relation to the Unconscious*, W. W. Norton & Company, 1990.
John Morreall, *The Philosophy of Humor and Laughter*, SUNY Press, 1986.

Stories and Logical Puzzles

Lewis Carroll, *Alice's Adventures in Wonderland*, and *Through the Looking Glass*, Penguin Classics, 2015.
Peter Heath, *The Philosopher's Alice*, St. Martin's Press, 1974.
Raymond Smullyan, *What Is the Name of This Book?*, Dover Publications, 2011; *This Book Needs No Title*, Touchstone, 1986.

Index